PRAISE FOR

Something Extra

"I have known and worked with Lisa Nichols for over ten years now, and she practices what she preaches in her work and her community. Lisa has captured the 'extra' that turns good leaders into great ones—and she shows us how to cultivate it. A very worthy read!"

MAXINE CLARK

Founder of Build-A-Bear Workshop and CEO of Clark-Fox Family Foundation

"Each human being is specially created by God to bring a unique 'something extra' to the world around us. Lisa Nichols has interviewed hundreds of accomplished guests for her podcast. Now she has compiled some of the best insights from those conversations and added her own personal nuggets of wisdom, along with life lessons from her delightfully inspiring daughter, Ally. This book will give you a lot to think about and apply in any vocation."

JIM DALY

President of Focus on the Family

"In *Something Extra*, Lisa has created a wonderful combination of compelling narratives. It is both immensely readable and a great reference tool."

PATRICK LENCIONI

Founder & President of The Table Group

"Lisa Nichols is a values-driven leader who dedicates herself to making a positive difference in all aspects of her life and work. This book offers insight into Lisa's leadership philosophy. It encourages readers to reflect on the traits she calls "something extra," the often intangible, yet essential characteristics that distinguish the most impactful leaders from the rest. It's a helpful resource for anyone seeking to cultivate not just effective, but truly inspiring leadership."

KATHY MAZZARELLA

Chairman, President & CEO of Graybar

"Lisa Nichols is a gift to everyone who knows her! In *Something Extra*, she has given us a gift, allowing us to learn from her story and from many of the leaders she's met on her journey. Thanks, Lisa, for serving each of us so well as we attempt to steward our 'Something Extra!'"

MARK MILLER

Former Vice President of High Performance Leadership at Chick-fil-A, Inc.;
Wall Street Journal *Bestselling Author of* Culture Rules

"*Something Extra* is a dynamic and unique exploration of leadership principles, wrapped with real-world stories and biblical truths, that will inspire you to new heights. Lisa's heart for people amplifies each topic in a meaningful Christ-centered way, encouraging me always to be purpose-full. In aerospace parlance, this book made me 'take flight'!"

DENNIS MUILENBURG

Retired President & CEO of Boeing

"Lisa has authored a brilliant, insightful, and actionable blueprint for life. In sharing personal stories from her family, from phenomenal leaders she's interviewed on her podcast, and from personal insights she's learned along the way, she lays out a brilliant guide on not only becoming the best version of ourselves, but also elevating the lives of those we encounter along the way."

JOHN O'LEARY

Bestselling Author of On Fire *and* In Awe

"Lisa Nichols guides the reader through deeper experiences and questions of daily leadership. Once you read *Something Extra*, you will be a better leader of yourself and your organization."

HORST SCHULZE

Cofounder & Former President of The Ritz-Carlton Hotel Company

"The word 'extra' means something very different to Lisa Nichols and her family. And now she shares with all of us what 'something extra' truly looks like. We will all live, love, and lead differently because of this special book. Lisa is truly an 'extra' gift of influence."

TOMMY SPAULDING

New York Times *Bestselling Author of* The Heart Led Leader *and* The Gift of Influence

"ONLY FOR THOSE SERIOUSLY SEEKING LEADERSHIP SKILLS. Lisa Nichols knows her subject and shares it all in *Something Extra*. Anyone fully committed to leadership with a heart for others will benefit from absorbing the information and incorporating it into their own personal and professional lives."

TOM ZIGLAR

CEO of Zig Ziglar Corporation

SOMETHING EXTRA

Uncover
Your Strengths.
Unlock
Your Potential.
Unleash
Your Impact.

LISA NICHOLS

Published by StoryBuilders Press

979-8-89833-003-3 - Paperback

979-8-89833-004-0 - Hardcover

979-8-89833-005-7 - eBook

979-8-89833-006-4 - Audiobook

Cover and Interior DNA Strand Artwork by Morgan Cochran

CONTENTS

FOREWORD

Writing this foreword for my wife, Lisa Nichols, and her book, *Something Extra*, is not just an honor—it's deeply personal. Since we have shared a lifetime, I've had a front-row seat to her remarkable journey.

We've been friends since elementary school, dated through high school and college, and married for over 40 years. Along the way, we've raised three children and now enjoy the incredible gift of being grandparents.

Over the decades, I've watched Lisa grow from a curious and compassionate friend into a remarkable woman, wife, mother, business leader, speaker, podcaster, and now, author.

What has always remained constant is Lisa's deep love for people and her unquenchable curiosity to understand what makes them thrive. That curiosity, paired with her passion for helping others, is the heartbeat of this book.

In our experience, successful people can often point to a few key strengths–such as resilience, empathy, discipline, or vision— that contributed significantly to their success at various points in their journey.

Describing these strengths as a "something extra" was inspired by our daughter, Ally, who was born with Down syndrome, which amounts to every cell of her body having an extra chromosome. While that extra chromosome brings challenges, it also tends to give individuals an extraordinarily tender and loving spirit. The joy and love that flows through Ally warms the hearts of everyone she meets. That's her "something extra." You'll learn a lot more about Ally in the pages to come.

This book will inspire you as you discover and cultivate the "something extras" you need most for roles you play, whether in business or at home. As I read each page, I thought, "Given that same situation, I want to learn to be more like that." I'm confident you will find this book valuable.

Lisa, you've dreamed of writing your book since your parents bought you that small blue typewriter at age seven. I can picture Gene and June smiling from above, so proud of the woman you've become and the light you continue to share.

With all my love and admiration,

Greg

THE HEART BEHIND
SOMETHING EXTRA

**I praise you because I am fearfully
and wonderfully made.**

PSALM 139:14

E ach of us has been entrusted by God with something
extraordinary—a divine gift designed to impact
the world in a way only we can. Just as a gift holds no
value if it remains unopened, our God-given gifts were
meant to be discovered, nurtured, and shared. When
we faithfully unwrap what He has placed within us, we
become vessels of His love, grace, and light.

The world desperately needs our gifts—not for our own sakes but to reflect God's glory and to bless others. This isn't a new concept, but in becoming a mother to our daughter Ally, I have seen this truth illustrated firsthand. Born with an extra chromosome, Ally has taught our family more about joy, resilience, and unconditional love than we could have ever thought possible. In our family, we say that Ally has *something extra*—a beautiful reminder that what sets us apart is often what makes us shine the brightest.

This book is born from that belief. It's a collection of the most powerful lessons I've gathered from remarkable leaders who, like Ally, carry their own something extra. Their stories have changed the way I live and lead. And now, in sharing them with you, I want to invite you to also discover your own something extra.

Thank you for being here. I know you have many choices for how you spend your time, and it means so much to me that you're choosing to spend a little of it with me—and with the incredible leaders you'll meet on these pages.

My hope is that this book becomes a companion for you—a place you return to whenever you need encouragement, inspiration, or just a reminder that you are uniquely gifted for a purpose.

WHY *SOMETHING EXTRA*?

Each year in the United States, about 6,000 babies are born with an extra chromosome, making them a person with Down syndrome. If you've ever encountered someone with Down syndrome, you know they radiate something special—kindness, joy, and a beautiful authenticity that shines through in everything they do.

Ally was born in 1995, the youngest of our three children. You've probably heard it said that God doesn't always give you what you ask for but rather what you need. That has never been more true than in Ally's story—and ours.

When Ally was born, our world shifted. Like any parents, we had all the questions and concerns, wondering what the future would hold for her and for us. There was uncertainty, and there were moments of fear. But over time, our questions were answered, not with explanations but with joy, laughter, and love.

Ally has been one of the greatest blessings a parent could ever receive. She radiates light everywhere she goes and brings joy to every person she meets. Her presence has a way of softening hearts and opening eyes to what truly matters. We've heard this countless times: The best part of someone's week is simply spending time with Ally.

She has made our world better—transforming our entire family with her love, strength, and unique way she sees the beauty in everyone. Ally didn't just change our story; she redefined it. And we wouldn't have it any other way.

In her uniquely special way, Ally has taught us that what makes us different is often what makes us strong. Her extra chromosome became the lens through which I saw this powerful truth: *Every person has something extra.*

It may not show up on a chromosome chart, but it shows up in how we lead, love, create, and serve. That concept sparked the idea for the podcast *Something Extra*. There are hundreds, maybe thousands, of business and leadership podcasts already in production, but I could not stop thinking about the idea of "something extra." What if I could highlight all the ways that people are impacting the world in their fields of expertise, walks of life, or specific circumstances? What could I learn? What could I share?

The podcast launched in 2018 with an incredible interview with Maxine Clark whom you will meet later on. She was quickly followed by a wide variety of guests, including CEOs, entrepreneurs, philanthropists, educators, athletes, and adventurers—some of the world's most thoughtful leaders. I was honored as people shared their stories and hard-won life lessons.

Playing off the podcast title, I concluded each episode by asking my guest, "What's the something extra you believe every leader needs?"

As I interviewed amazing guest after amazing guest, I was inspired and encouraged by their answers. Curiosity. Gratitude. Vulnerability. Resilience. Humility. Vision. The list went on.

As I listened, I found myself thinking, *I wish more people could hear this, not just once but over and over again.* Wisdom like this deserves to be held onto, reflected upon, and shared.

Each conversation was remarkable in its own right—incredible stories of personal triumph, business acumen, and bold leadership. And each conversation confirmed that the most impactful leaders carry something extra that sets them apart.

This book is my attempt to curate the best of what I've learned. I've taken some of the most often-mentioned "something extras" and highlighted various podcast guests who embody those leadership principles in a unique and unforgettable way. It's still only a sampling. We're over 300 episodes in and still going strong.

My hope is that these stories will inspire you to uncover your own strengths, unlock your potential, and ultimately unleash your impact.

HOW TO USE THIS BOOK

You'll notice that each chapter highlights a single leadership principle or character quality, and each chapter stands alone. You can read the book cover to cover (the compelling stories will make it hard to put it down), or you can jump to the topics that most resonate.

I am a big fan of books that teach, inspire, and cause me to take action. I love to underline, highlight, and jot down questions or insights in the margins. I prefer books that keep me thinking for days. My prayer is that I've written that kind of book for you.

Each chapter ends with reflection questions and activities to help you not just read but put into practice the wisdom you encounter in the chapter. You may take a look at the thorough reflection sections and think, *There's no way I can get through all these questions.* That's on purpose. This book is meant to be a companion, not a textbook.

Let the insights marinate over time, come back to the chapters that resonate, and revisit the action steps. Don't feel like you need to rush to finish this book. Growth isn't a race; it's a journey of discovery and reflection. Take your time. Pause when a thought stirs something in you. Return to the chapters again and again. Let this book work on you slowly, the way real, meaningful change always does.

Throughout the book, you'll see short sidebars called *Ally's Something Extra.* These are anecdotes from our life with Ally—snapshots that show how pure joy, perseverance, and kindness can transform ordinary moments into extraordinary ones.

Ally's presence will be a gentle reminder throughout these pages that true leadership doesn't always look like standing at the front of the room or holding a title. Sometimes it looks like a smile, a kind word, or a willingness to see the best in someone else.

Her life reminds us daily that the most important leadership lessons are often the simplest.

YOUR INVITATION

As you turn the pages ahead, you'll meet leaders from all walks of life, each one sharing a piece of wisdom that helped shape who they are today. Some lessons will challenge you. Some will comfort you. All are meant to stir something within you.

As you reflect on your own life and leadership, let me encourage you to be openhearted and courageous. More than ever, the world needs what you have to offer. Take time to pause and ponder this: What is your *something extra*?

I am honored to walk alongside you. Let's begin.

empowering

empathetic

adaptable

inspiring

approach

PART ONE

IT STARTS ON THE INSIDE

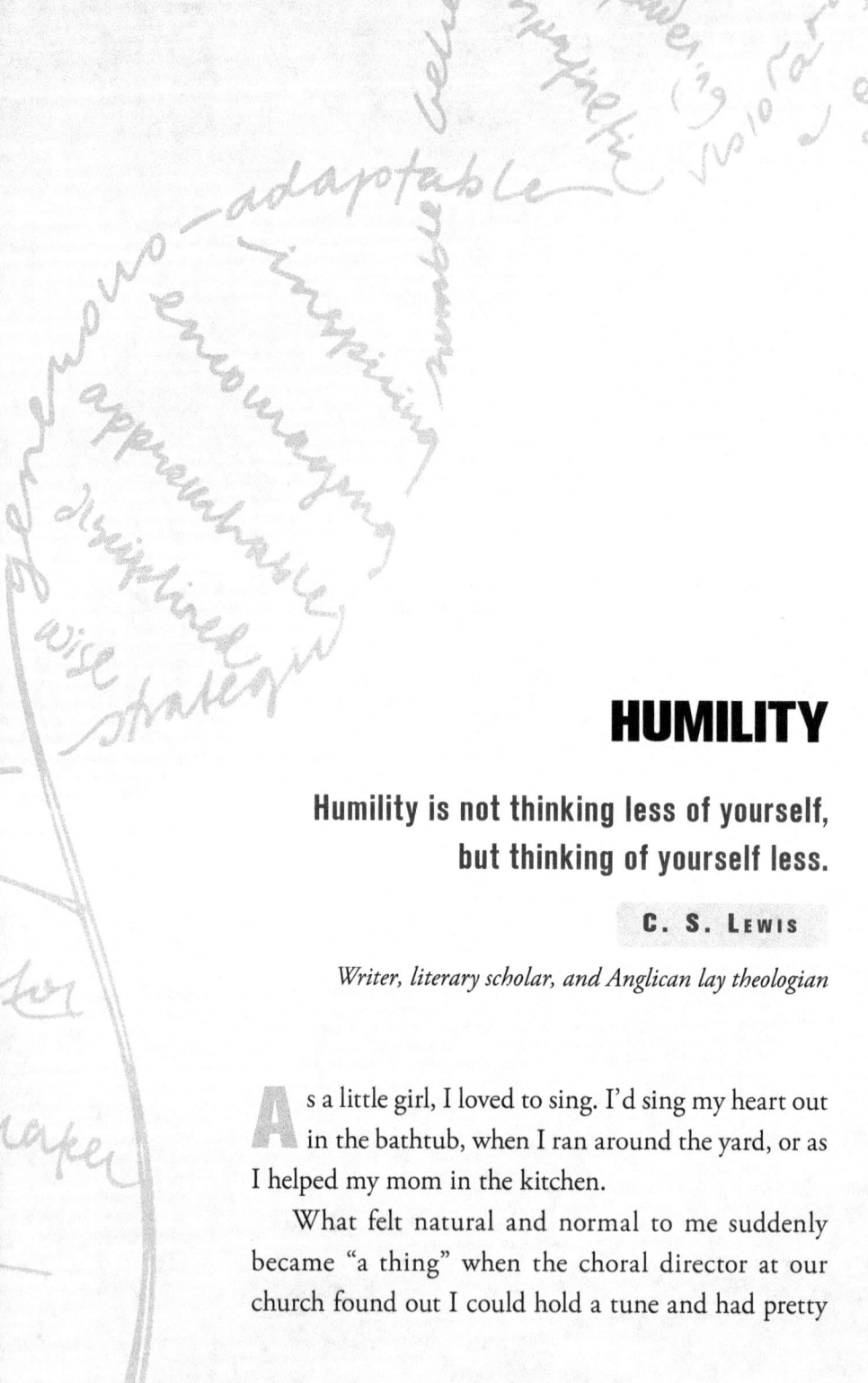

HUMILITY

Humility is not thinking less of yourself, but thinking of yourself less.

C. S. LEWIS

Writer, literary scholar, and Anglican lay theologian

As a little girl, I loved to sing. I'd sing my heart out in the bathtub, when I ran around the yard, or as I helped my mom in the kitchen.

What felt natural and normal to me suddenly became "a thing" when the choral director at our church found out I could hold a tune and had pretty good tone quality, even at four years old. She made it her mission to develop my singing voice and share it with others.

That often meant singing solos in church, at first standing proudly on a small wooden stool, my blond pigtails swaying as I looked out over the congregation and sang a simple "Jesus Loves Me." As my sweet, little-girl voice grew and developed, I moved on to hymns and more complicated arrangements. As a teenager, I competed in local and state music competitions.

The year I was sixteen, I received the highest score, beating even older students, including my angel-voiced role model. I was amazed and thrilled, and I began to think pretty highly of myself and my beautiful voice.

Shortly after that victory, I learned the value of remaining humble even in the wake of success when I was involved in a car accident. In the crash, my body was thrown into the steering wheel, and my throat took the majority of the impact. I emerged from the car gasping, crying, and unable to speak. I was devastated. Not only could I not speak, but what about singing? Would I ever sing again?

I had surgery, which allowed me to speak, and my mom drove me to a voice rehabilitation coach twice a week for a whole year to help me recover my singing voice. I can now sing, but I never regained my high soprano register.

At a very young age, I learned about humility in a tangible, obvious way.

WHAT IS HUMILITY?

The Bible cautions us against thinking more highly of ourselves than we should, reminding us that God opposes the proud. Sometimes we start to believe the headlines or what others say about how great we are. If we're not careful to keep ourselves grounded, that praise can quietly become pride—and pride is often the first step toward a leader's downfall. Humility, on the other hand, opens the door to wisdom, connection, and lasting impact.

When I reflect on humble leaders who have left an indelible mark on my career and life, Don Imholz immediately comes to mind. We first crossed paths when I was fresh out of college and working at McDonnell Douglas. Don was my boss's boss—several levels removed from me in the organizational chart—but what stood out was his extraordinary willingness to see people, no matter their title or tenure.

Don probably didn't realize it at the time, but he became a formative mentor in my journey. Without any formal designation or fanfare, he invited me to meetings, gave me a seat at the table, and modeled what it meant to lead with quiet confidence and inclusive wisdom. I watched, learned, and soaked in every interaction.

Don once said, "I always tried to surround myself with people smarter than me." That humble mindset is exactly what made him such a magnetic and trusted leader. Whether he was leading major IT transformations at Boeing or later guiding Centene through explosive growth, he had a rare ability to uplift others by simply believing in them, inviting them in, and leading with humility.

He believed that the health of an organization could be measured by how quickly bad news rose to the top. And with that, he created a culture of trust, summed up best by his powerful reminder: "Come to me early, you have a coach. Come to me late, you have a judge."

From that early start of my career until now, Don and I have remained friends, and I'm still learning from him every time we're together. Don taught me that great leaders don't just lead organizations; they leave fingerprints on people's lives. And if we're lucky, those fingerprints stay with us forever.

The older I get, the more I realize how little I can truly accomplish on my own. As a young girl—and even as a young professional—I didn't fully grasp this. I believed that if I just worked harder and smarter, I could achieve anything I set my mind to. But with that mindset, it's easy to slip into pride, thinking that success is solely the result of your own ingenuity and effort. Over time, I've learned that true strength and lasting success come not from striving alone but from surrendering and relying on Someone far greater than myself.

Even now, years after my car accident and thanks to the influence of leaders like Don, I am reminded that every skill and talent I have, whether it's singing or my ability to lead, is a gift from God. Life has a way of teaching us that collaboration, support from others, and faith play significant roles in our achievements.

Embracing humility allows me to appreciate the contributions of others and recognize that we are all interconnected in our journeys. It fosters a sense of gratitude and encourages a collaborative spirit, reminding me that every success is a collective effort.

I loved talking to Sean Swarner, an inspiring adventurer who has successfully climbed the seven highest mountain summits in the world and skied to both the North and South Poles. He emphasized that he has *never* reached a summit alone even though he is the one placing the flag on the mountain.

It has been a team effort every time.

HUMILITY IN PRACTICE

Humility is about understanding your place in the world. Cultivating humility is an intentional and ongoing process that involves self-awareness, a willingness to learn, and a commitment to valuing others.

None of us knows it all, and we need each other. As I gauge my motives and my actions, I often ask myself, *Is this humility or hubris?*

> ➤ Do I act as though I'm the most important person in the room? That's something a person with hubris might do.

> ➤ Do I insist on having the first and last word? Hubris would.

> ➤ Do I care about getting credit for an idea? Again, that's hubris talking.

> ➤ Do I feel compelled to be the center of attention? A person with hubris would.

While I can't claim to have fully mastered humility, it is a value I try to keep front and center. Humility is an ongoing exercise in self-awareness, and it shapes much of how I aim to lead and serve. And if I don't remain humble, it's only a matter of time before I am humbled. So many leaders achieve success, meet their goals, impact the world, and then fall because they begin to think more about themselves and their greatness than the people they serve.

Simple habits in daily life can help foster humility. I've learned to pause and let others speak, even when I have plenty to say. (I *always* have something to say since my brain is usually running 200 miles an hour.) I try to ask questions, inviting others to share their thoughts without feeling the need to offer my own opinion right away. Humility starts with truly hearing others and being open to perspectives different from my own.

Humble people also acknowledge their limitations and invite feedback. Humble leaders surround themselves with people who will keep them grounded. Constructive criticism doesn't always feel good in the moment, but if approached with a growth mindset, it can be really valuable.

Humble people realize they don't have to have all the answers. In fact, Jeff Henderson, president of the FOR Company, a professional training and coaching company, told me, "I think every leader should say these words on a very consistent basis: 'I don't know.'" Admitting your limitations is a sign of strength, not weakness. Being vulnerable gives others permission to admit their own weaknesses and pursue their own success.

Danny Ludeman, the late chairman and CEO at Concordance, a nonprofit organization that assists individuals in successfully reintegrating into society from prison, told me he thinks the primary job of a leader is helping other individuals in your organization become the best they can be. Of course, that requires humility as well as honesty. He said we may want people to judge us on our good intentions, but they actually can only judge us by our actions. Danny exemplified this through his life and work. His legacy lives on in the countless lives changed through Concordance, and I'm deeply grateful for the wisdom he shared with me and so many others.

A humble leader makes others feel seen, valued, and understood. Championing others' successes and appreciating others' contributions reminds me that no accomplishment is truly a solo act.

This is true in my personal life, and it's been true in our business. To truly succeed as a company, we need everyone's unique contributions because, like Sean Swarner says, who wants to reach the top alone?

LEADERSHIP LEGACY

I recently had the privilege of attending the annual CEO Forum, an incredible gathering of faith-driven CEOs and leaders committed to supporting one another in becoming spiritual statespeople in the marketplace. The CEO Forum, now a 30-year-old organization, has been a beacon for those seeking to lead with both excellence and purpose, integrating their faith into their leadership.

One of the most inspiring moments of the event was when Mike Duke, the retired CEO of Walmart, was honored with the prestigious Mac McQuiston Distinguished Leader Award. Mike is widely respected for his unwavering commitment to putting people and relationships first.

As speaker after speaker shared their personal stories, a common theme emerged. Mike had not only made a lasting impact on the organization but on the lives of countless individuals as well. And what trait was cited repeatedly as the cornerstone of Mike's leadership? Humility.

Mike's ability to lead with grace, always valuing others and lifting them up, left an indelible mark on those who worked with him. It was a powerful reminder that true leadership is not about titles or accomplishments but about how we treat the people around us and the legacy of humble care we leave behind.

Reflection:

1. What is your personal definition of true humility? How does it differ from simply minimizing yourself? Reflect on how humility aligns with confidence and service without diminishing your self-worth.

2. When was the last time you prioritized someone else's needs over your own? How did it make you feel? Consider what this experience taught you about the balance between humility and self-care.

3. How do you respond when you are praised or recognized for your work? Reflect on whether your reaction demonstrates gratitude and humility or veers toward self-centeredness or discomfort.

4. What role does humility play in your relationships? Examine whether practicing humility strengthens connections with others or highlights areas where ego may be creating distance.

5. What specific moments in your life have humbled you? How did they shape your character? Reflect on what these moments revealed about your strengths, vulnerabilities, and the value of humility in personal growth.

6. Romans 12:3 analysis: What does it mean to you in practical terms to not think more highly of yourself than you should?

 **Action:**

Hubris vs. Humility Tracker: Create a checklist of hubris and humility traits, and assess yourself daily. Commit to shifting your actions toward humility.

ACTION	IS IT HUBRIS?	IS IT HUMILITY?

Gift Inventory Exercise: Consider this list of talents and abilities. Circle the ten that you find are personal strengths of yours. Reframe your perspective that these are gifts rather than accomplishments and reflect on how you can use them to serve others.

70 STRENGTHS

Adaptability

Analytical Thinking

Assertiveness

Attention to Detail

Authenticity

Calmness
under Pressure

Charisma

Collaboration

Commitment

Communication

Compassion

Confidence

Conflict Resolution

Consistent Performance	Organizational Skills
Creativity	Patience
Critical Thinking	Perseverance
Decision Making	Persuasiveness
Delegation	Persuasion
Dependability	Positivity
Determination	Practicality
Discipline	Problem Solving
Emotional Intelligence	Productivity
Entrepreneurship	Public Speaking
Ethical Judgment	Reliability
Flexibility	Resilience
Goal-Oriented	Resourcefulness
Gratitude	Risk Management
Growth Mindset	Self-awareness
Honesty	Self-discipline
Humor	Self-motivation
Initiative	Sense of Responsibility
Integrity	Strategic Thinking
Interpersonal Skills	Stress Management
Leadership	Team Player
Listening	Time Management
Logical Reasoning	Tolerance
Loyalty	Trustworthiness
Negotiation	Visionary Thinking
Open-mindedness	Work Ethic
Optimism	Writing Skills

Connection:

Constructive Feedback Seeking: Ask a mentor or peer for honest feedback about your behavior and leadership style. Reflect on their insights.

Humble Leader Interview: Interview a leader you admire for their humility. Ask about their practices for staying grounded and valuing others.

Shared Credit Acknowledgment: During a group project or task, intentionally acknowledge others' contributions publicly.

Humility Accountability Partner: Pair with a colleague or friend to share weekly insights on practicing humility and encourage each other.

Growth:

Humility Growth Plan: Write actionable steps to practice humility such as seeking feedback, pausing before speaking, or serving others selflessly.

Selfless Act of Service: Do something anonymously to help someone else, whether it's paying for a stranger's coffee or volunteering without recognition.

Silent-Day Challenge: Spend one day intentionally refraining from giving opinions unless directly asked. Focus entirely on listening. Journal how you felt throughout the day.

Ally's Something Extra

Ally is always the first to raise a glass, offer a heartfelt toast, or warmly welcome others at an event. She embraces every opportunity to speak in public with a confidence that is both natural and unshakable. As her parents, Greg and I believe this comes from her deep humility. She doesn't elevate herself above others, so the fear of failure simply doesn't exist for her. She isn't held back by concerns of looking *less than* in anyone's eyes because she never placed herself above in the first place. Isn't that a beautiful way to be?

Something Extra Podcast

- ► Danny Ludeman, episode 18
- ► Don Imholz, episode 70
- ► Jeff Henderson, episode 121
- ► Sean Swarner, episode 307

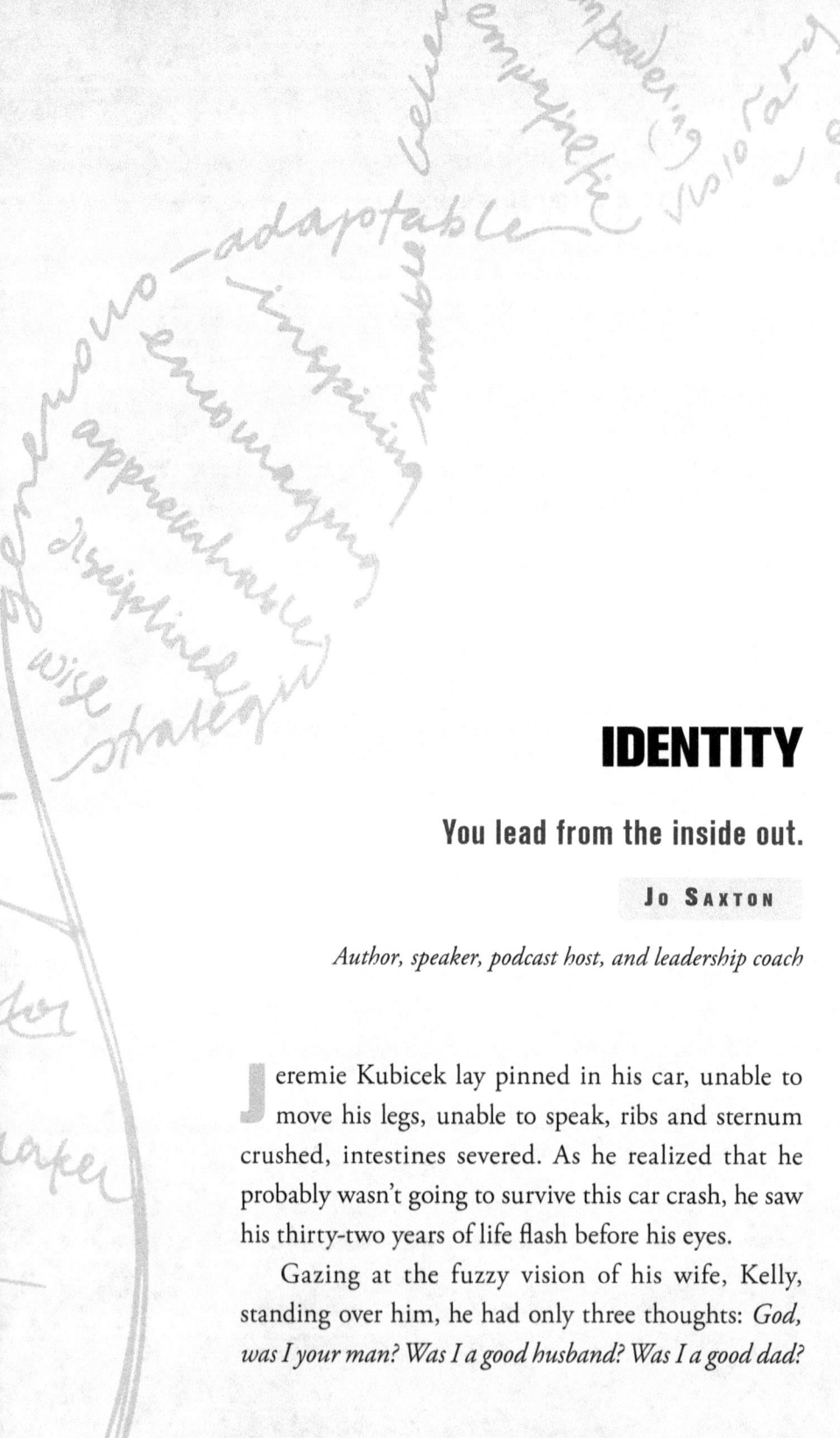

IDENTITY

You lead from the inside out.

Jo Saxton

Author, speaker, podcast host, and leadership coach

Jeremie Kubicek lay pinned in his car, unable to move his legs, unable to speak, ribs and sternum crushed, intestines severed. As he realized that he probably wasn't going to survive this car crash, he saw his thirty-two years of life flash before his eyes.

Gazing at the fuzzy vision of his wife, Kelly, standing over him, he had only three thoughts: *God, was I your man? Was I a good husband? Was I a good dad?*

At this critical point, Jeremie wasn't thinking about the businesses he'd created or the financial success he'd had. In the moments when it seemed like it was all over, what was really important became crystal clear.

Jeremie and Kelly were in Mexico for a much-needed break before Jeremie dove into a startup business venture. Unfortunately, their tropical getaway was interrupted by category three Hurricane Isidore.

As the storm began to blow in, Jeremie and Kelly took a taxi from their beach resort to an inland hotel in downtown Cancun to hunker down for the night. Just one block from their destination, a drunk driver out joyriding in the hurricane winds slammed into their taxi, crushing the side of the car and much of Jeremie's body.

Prior to this accident, Jeremie might have identified himself as a successful business person. After all, he'd spent his twenties cofounding a business, working for a national distributor, creating multiple dot-com businesses, working with a private equity group to purchase dozens of companies, and currently poised to start a company called GiANT.

His identity might have been caught up in what he did, but as he faced the end of his life, he was less concerned about *what he'd done* and more aware of *who he was*.

His core identity came sharply into focus.

A SOLID FOUNDATION

Like Jeremie, you may have reached a pivotal point where you were forced to consider your true identity. At its core, identity is rooted in self-awareness. Who are we when all the externals are stripped away?

I have had the privilege of talking with hundreds of amazing people on the *Something Extra* podcast. Not a single person has the same story. My guests differ in core values, beliefs, life experiences, and cultural backgrounds. All those different aspects that make up a person's life mold and shape their core identity.

One of my podcast guests, Rich McClure, refers to personal identity as the foundation from which we live out our lives every day in our choices and actions. Rich's story includes leadership in the public and private sectors as well as in philanthropic and community efforts.

Rich began his career in politics as deputy chief of staff and assistant to Governor Jim Thompson of Illinois. He served as cabinet-level director of Illinois' Central Department of Management Services. From 1985 until 1992, he was chief of staff for Missouri Governor and former U.S. Attorney General John Ashcroft.

For years, Rich was able to point to his fancy office in the state capitol or hand out a business card with the title that read Chief of Staff, State of Missouri, Office of the Governor as an obvious statement of his identity. That all changed when he left the governor's office and entered the private sector corporate world.

That career shift forced him to recognize the vital importance of having a solid identity foundation *outside* his work title. Work comes and goes, but who you are on the inside stays.

Retired professional basketball player Jayson Wells told me the same thing. He said the main reason people struggle with their purpose is because they don't know who they are. When Jayson decided to move on from basketball, he had to work through that change in identity. If he wasn't a basketball player, then who was he?

He had to find his identity in something other than the sport he played. He asked questions like these:

- What am I passionate about?
- What sets me apart from everybody else?
- How do I overcome adversity?

He said, "When the ball stops bouncing, it's still going to be a transition, but what I found is if you're rooted in self-awareness and in who you are and what your identity is outside of the game you play, it makes that transition smoother."

Whether politics, athletics, or business, your identity cannot be solely attached to what you do because positions and titles change.

AUTHENTICITY BUILDS TRUST

I am a wife, a mother, a grandmother, a friend, and a business leader. I have not always been all those things. My life circumstances have dictated different roles at different times. Regardless of my position, I find my solid foundation in my faith. At the root of everything, I know and believe that I am a daughter of the King. This foundation of God as my Father shapes how I see myself in all other roles, relationships, and responsibilities.

Over the years as my titles have changed, I have had to consider my identity and the impact it has on how I lead. My faith gives me a sense of purpose and perspective. My hope is that people under my leadership see that in me and trust that any decisions I make or advice I give stems from that solid cornerstone.

I often say that as the leader goes, so goes the organization. That applies to all of us whether it's in your home and family or a Fortune 500 company. We all lead in some way, and every leader needs a clear personal identity in order to best serve the people in their sphere of influence.

Many people struggle with identity because they let external voices and influences define them rather than rooting their identity in their core values and beliefs. A leader has to understand who they are before they can lead other people in an authentic way because what you believe about your identity affects how you make decisions, how you interact with others, and how you live out your purpose. It's the foundation for everything else. The key is finding that voice of truth about who you really are rather than letting the noise of the world define your identity. I have found that this is an ongoing process of self-discovery and living with authenticity.

Do you know who you are—who you really are on the inside? Maybe you're a coach, a parent, a friend, or a business owner. Whatever your role, whatever your level of influence, living from a solid foundation makes all the difference.

TRUE FREEDOM

Jeremie Kubicek breathed his last breath and was gone. For three or four minutes he saw himself floating above the car in a slow fade. He was at total peace, in no pain.

But amazingly, Jeremie Kubicek did not die in Mexico. He was given a second life. Over the next seven days, a series of miracles occurred that reshaped his worldview and his entire life.

After months of rehabilitation, his body healed, and he did go on to start his new company, but he did it with a drastically different perspective. He already had a background of faith, but this experience in Mexico made it all come to life in ways it hadn't before. It highlighted the deep importance of Jeremie's personal identity and his calling to serve others.

Today Jeremie is a *Wall Street Journal* bestselling author, thought leader, and entrepreneur. He has cofounded over twenty-five businesses and written more than half a dozen books. He regularly speaks to groups all over the world on the topic of transformational leadership.

But Jeremie knows those accomplishments don't define who he really is at his core. Every day Jeremie goes through a mental and spiritual practice he refers to as a "call up" that grounds him in his true identity. *God, remind me who I am today.*

And in a profound, loving way, God speaks. *You are a liberator. A freedom fighter. A creator. An encourager. That's who you are, Jeremie. Let's go.*

Calling himself into the position and mission he has each day has been life-changing. Knowing his identity at the core enables Jeremie to lean into his gifts, use his talents, and bring life to those around him.

Knowing and living in your true identity brings freedom.

You're free to be yourself. You're free to lead in an authentic way. You're free to pursue the purpose you were made for.

Reflection:

....

1. How would you rate your understanding of your identity on a scale of 1 to 10? Why?

2. What is your personal definition of "identity"? Write your definition of identity in your own words. Compare it to a formal dictionary definition.

3. In what ways have your culture, family, or societal expectations shaped your sense of identity? Create a list of influences— upbringing, culture, education, personal experience—and estimate how much each has shaped your identity.

4. Are there aspects of your identity that conflict with how you were raised or taught to think?

5. How do you perceive the difference between your work identity and personal identity? Do you see yourself differently in public versus private settings? Why?

6. How does spiritual identity play a role in your sense of self? What does being a child of God (or another spiritual identity) mean to you?

7. What is one aspect of your identity that you wish others better understood and appreciated?

 **Action:**

In this Venn diagram, compare your work identity and personal identity. Where do they overlap?

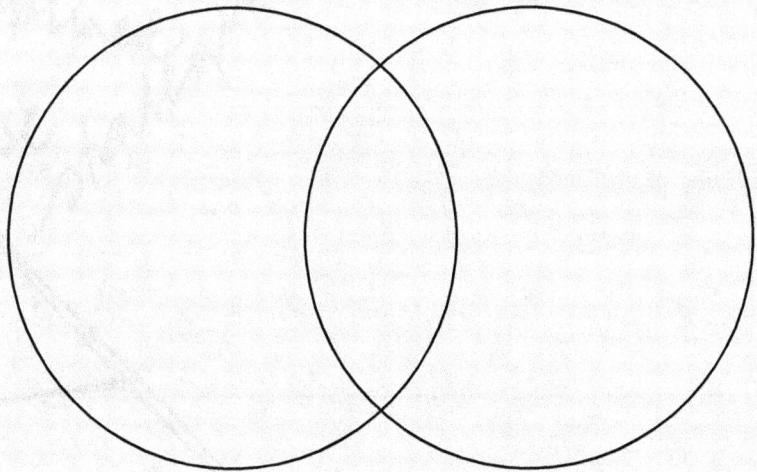

In this T-chart, make a list of roles you play—sibling, friend, leader—and then describe how each contributes to your overall identity.

	LIST OF ROLES	HOW IT CONTRIBUTES TO MY IDENTITY
	1. 2. 3.	

Using this Daily Schedule, assess how you spend your time at each hour of a normal workday. Check off whether that activity is a passion you love to do or an obligation you have to do. Reflect on the balance.

	DAILY ACTIVITY	PASSION	OBLIGATION
8 am		✓	✓
9 am			
10 am			
11 am			
12 pm			

Now fill out this monthly calendar with your events for the month. Put a star next to the events that are for you and your passions.

SUN	MON	TUE	WED	THU	FRI	SAT

Consider the word bank of identity markers on the following page. Select the top five most meaningful to you. Reflect on why they resonate.

► Which identity markers do you feel are positive? Which ones feel negative? Why?

► What assumptions or biases might you have about certain aspects of your identity?

PROFESSIONAL IDENTITY

WORD LIST

OVERVIEW: Which words represent your current professional identity? Which words represent your desired or aspirational professional identity? Circle or select the words that resonate with you currently. If there are words you aspire to but have not yet embodied in your work, put them in a separate list. Choose as many as you like, and feel free to add your own words too.

ACCELERATOR	BLENDER
ACHIEVER	BUILDER
ACTION TAKER	CAPTAIN
ACTIVATOR	CAREGIVER
ACTOR	CARTOGRAPHER
ADAPTER	CATCHER
AGENT	CATEGORIZER
ALLY	CHALLENGER
AMBASSADOR	CHAMPION
ANALYST	CHANGE-MAKER
ANCHOR	CHIEF
ARCHITECT	CITIZEN
ARTIST	COLLABORATOR
ASSESSOR	COMEDIAN
ASSISTANT	COMMUNICATOR
ATHLETE	CONDUCTOR
BALANCER	CONTROLLER
BALANCING	CRAFTSPERSON

CRAFTER	FELLOW
CREATOR	FILMMAKER
DENTIST	FIXER
DESIGNER	FOUNDER
DEVELOPER	FUELER
DIRECTOR	GAMER
DISRUPTOR	GATHERER
DREAMER	GATEKEEPER
EDUCATOR	GIVER
ENGINEER	GO GETTER
ENTHUSIAST	GUIDE
EVALUATOR	HEALER
EXPERIMENTER	HELPER
EXPLORER	HUMANIZER
FACILITATOR	ILLUMINATOR
FANATIC	INFLUENCER

 **Connection:**

Legacy Interview: Interview an elder—a family member, neighbor, or nursing home resident—about how they would like their life to be remembered. How would you like to be remembered by your family, friends, and community? Read obituaries and write your own. Reflect on how your current identity aligns with the legacy you want to leave behind.

Coffee Conversation: Ask a close friend or family member how they perceive your identity. Compare their perception to your own self-view. Write about any differences and insights.

Growth:

....

Visualization Exercise: Picture your ideal future self. Write or draw who you want to be in five, ten, or twenty years.

Goal-Setting Template: Map out actionable steps to grow into your envisioned self. Include short-term and long-term goals.

Personal Identity Statement: Craft your own statement about your identity. This should reflect who you are, what you value, and the person you aspire to become.

 Something Extra Podcast

....

- ► Rich McClure, episode 87
- ► Jayson Wells, episode 88
- ► Jo Saxton, episode 166
- ► Jeremie Kubicek, episode 271

SOUL-CARE

You can't live life at warp speed
without warping your soul.

LANCE WITT

Author, speaker, and founder of Replenish Ministries

Lance Witt was in a crisis. As a pastor at Saddleback
Church in 2006, his job was both intoxicating
and demanding. Four years before, senior pastor Rick
Warren had written the bestselling book *The Purpose
Driven Life* that catapulted Saddleback into a period
of explosive growth. Rick became an international

celebrity seemingly overnight. People flocked to the church, and soon a number of spin-off programs sprang to life to meet the need and interest. The impact was immense.

Lance was in charge of leading the 40 Days of Purpose and 40 Days of Community campaigns. In many ways, it was his dream job. Many lives were being impacted. Ultimately, both nationally and internationally, more than 25,000 churches joined Saddleback in the 40 Days of Purpose campaign.

It was exciting and also exhausting. Lance loved it, but it was also destroying him. The pace of his life was out of control. He was burned out, his family was feeling the strain, and he knew he had not been leading himself well. He told me, "I was weary, emotionally empty, and spiritually dry. I was feeding others while starving my own soul."

He could not continue. In 2006, Lance made the difficult decision to step down. He did not have another ministry to go to or another job lined up. He just knew something had to change. He was called to be a leader, but he had to figure out a way to do it with a healthy soul.

SELF-CARE OR SOUL-CARE?

The concept of self-care is nothing new. Every time I travel by airplane, I am reminded of the importance of putting on my own oxygen mask before helping others. You've likely heard the adage that you can't pour from an empty cup. Talking with Lance, though, helped me realize that soul-care is something more than what we usually think of as self-care.

Rather than simply soothing ourselves with a short break from activity or a "me-time" indulgence, soul-care implies a more holistic approach to nurturing our inner health, emotional resilience, and spiritual well-being. Soul-care is something deeper. It is about reconnecting with your core values, purpose, and sense of peace.

A lack of soul-care shows up in various ways such as emotional emptiness, spiritual dryness, relationship problems, and a general feeling of being overwhelmed. There's no doubt the 24/7 noise and distractions of the world are soul-crushing. Leaders all over the world say, "I am so crazy busy. I'm exhausted. I'm overwhelmed. I'm overcommitted. I have no margin in my life."

Tad Edwards, chairman, CEO, and president of Benjamin F. Edwards, a national wealth management firm, told me that when he started his business, he went about ten years without one day off. He took vacations, but even as he walked the beach, he had his phone in hand to be in touch by text or email. When he finally took a couple weeks off completely away from his work, he came face to face with his humanity. The pace at which he was living was not sustainable. Regular time away was required for him to be able to bring his whole self to every part of his life. He needed it, his family needed it, and his team needed it.

Unfortunately, we don't always recognize the symptoms until we're deep into mental and physical burnout, our relationships are strained, and we're making poor decisions. We feel like we're teetering on the edge. Like Lance and Tad, we know something has to change.

HOW TO TEND TO YOUR SOUL

We manage our time, schedules, and calendars. We manage our finances and businesses. But our souls are not things we manage.

Souls require tending and nurturing. Rhythms of work and rest, activity, and relaxation feed the soul.

For Lance Witt, tending his soul meant embracing the concept of *selah*, a Hebrew word that means pause or intermission. Lance suggests a weekly intermission called a Sabbath, twenty-four hours dedicated to rest, and he also tries to schedule daily intermissions between meetings. Each week he schedules time on his calendar simply to think and process. The concept of *selah* offers a regular respite from the rat race.

Most of us are driven to keep going and be productive, but we rarely associate rest with productivity. The truth is that regular breaks, sleep, sabbaticals, and vacations are all essential for long-term soul health and success.

In addition to now taking real vacations, Tad Edwards also exercises, reads books, and spends time in prayer and Bible reading every day. That time of spiritual nurturing has become a foundational part of his life.

For me, soul-care requires a daily commitment. Each morning, I start my day making a cup of coffee, grabbing my Bible and journal, and spending intentional time in God's Word, meditation, and prayer. This practice sets the tone for my day, grounding me in God's presence and purpose.

When I skip this time, I feel off-center as if something vital is missing. These moments help me refocus on what matters most to God, aligning my heart with His purposes rather than relying on my own agenda. Nurturing my soul infuses the tasks and activities of my day with deeper meaning and eternal significance and enables me to approach my work and relationships with greater clarity, purpose, and love.

In addition to my daily practice, I also spend time reflecting at the end of each year. Taking time to reflect on where I've been and how I've lived is essential for personal growth, alignment, and renewal.

During this reflection, I ask myself these key questions:

- Have I stayed true to my core values?

- Did my actions and decisions align with the principles I hold dear?

- Are there areas of my life that need adjustment for the year ahead?

- Should I let go of activities that drain my soul or invest more in those that nurture and inspire me?

This intentional pause allows me to celebrate progress, acknowledge areas for growth, and realign with what truly matters as I move forward.

Jillian Tedesco, founder and CEO of Fit-Flavors, also refers to taking care of her soul and spirit as a grounding practice—something that keeps her healthy and energized. She, too, spends time reading the Bible and taking part in activities that fill her up. She finds that hot yoga at the gym, cooking, and playing golf are restful and rejuvenating.

Community and connection are also important for soul-care. Slowing down enough to truly be present with people and cultivating deep friendships where you can be fully known are vital. Mentors, peers, support groups, or personal friends and family can all give us a sense of belonging and purpose outside of our work or achievements.

LEADERSHIP LONG HAUL

Today, Lance Witt leads a ministry called Replenish that is dedicated to helping people live and lead from a healthy soul. Lance encourages, challenges, and equips leaders through speaking, personal coaching, and writing books.

Effective leadership requires energy, vision, and empathy—all qualities that arise from a well-nourished soul. Leaders who care for their souls are less likely to experience burnout, isolation, and decision fatigue. They are in tune with their values and purpose and are able to lead others with insight and compassion rather than just plowing ahead to the next thing.

A healthy soul leads to greater energy and focus over time, even in challenging circumstances. Soul-care helps us sustain all we are called to be and do.

Reflection:

....

1. What is the difference between self-care and soul-care in your life? Reflect on how you currently define and practice self-care. How does soul-care go beyond physical or surface-level maintenance to nurture your inner health, values, and sense of purpose?

2. When was the last time you felt deeply at peace? What contributed to that feeling? Identify the elements (activities, people, environments) that helped create that peace. How can you intentionally bring more of these into your daily life?

3. What distractions or habits in your life are draining your soul? How can you reduce or eliminate them? Consider the noise, commitments, or routines that leave you feeling overwhelmed or disconnected. How would your life change if you shifted your focus to what truly feeds your soul?

4. Which relationships in your life currently nurture your soul? Which ones feel depleting? Reflect on how your interactions with others impact your emotional and spiritual well-being. What boundaries or changes could improve your relationships?

5. If you could strip away all external expectations, achievements, and roles, what would remain at the core of who you are? Explore the essence of your identity apart from your responsibilities or titles. How can you align your daily life more closely with this authentic self?

 **Action:**

....

Soul Symptoms Checklist: Reflect on any signs of soul neglect in your life such as emotional emptiness, exhaustion, or relationship strain. Note patterns or triggers.

Value Identification Exercise: Circle your top five personal values from this word bank of values. How do they currently guide your decisions and daily life? Where are they missing?

VALUES

Accountability	Contentment
Achievement	Contribution
Adaptability	Cooperation
Adventure	Courage
Altruism	Ethics
Ambition	Excellence
Authenticity	Fairness
Balance	Faith
Beauty	Family
Being the best	Financial stability
Belonging	Forgiveness
Career	Freedom
Caring	Friendship
Collaboration	Fun
Commitment	Future generations
Community	Generosity
Compassion	Giving back
Competence	Grace
Confidence	Gratitude
Connection	Growth

Harmony	Pride
Health	Recognition
Home	Reliability
Honesty	Resourcefulness
Hope	Self-respect
Humility	Serenity
Humor	Service
Inclusion	Simplicity
Kindness	Spirituality
Knowledge	Sportsmanship
Leadership	Stewardship
Learning	Success
Legacy	Teamwork
Leisure	Thrift
Love	Time
Loyalty	Tradition
Making a difference	Travel
Nature	Trust
Openness	Truth
Optimism	Understanding
Order	Uniqueness
Parenting	Usefulness
Patience	Vision
Patriotism	Vulnerability
Peace	Wealth
Perseverance	Well-being
Personal fulfillment	Wholeheartedness
Power	Wisdom

Nature Walk Assignment: Take a walk in a natural setting and focus on your surroundings. Journal three observations about how they make you feel.

Quiet Retreat: Spend thirty minutes in silence, away from distractions, and reflect on what your soul most needs right now—rest, inspiration, connection, or something else. Many of the most effective leaders I know build in rhythms of silent retreats for journaling and reflecting.

Soul-Care Toolkit: Create a list of go-to activities, books, or resources that consistently nurture your soul. Use them as a reference when you feel drained.

ACTIVITIES	BOOKS	RESOURCES
1.	1.	1.
2.	2.	2.

Connection:

Soulful Conversations: Share with a trusted friend or partner what nurtures your soul and invite them to do the same. Discuss ways to support each other's soul-care practices.

Community Engagement: Volunteer for an activity that aligns with your values such as helping at a local shelter or mentoring someone in need. Reflect on how giving enriches your own soul.

Shared Meal Reflection: Host a dinner where everyone shares a moment of gratitude or a recent experience that nourished their soul.

An "I Love You, My Friend" Letter: Write a letter to someone important to you about what soul-care means to you and how you hope they'll prioritize it in their life.

 ## Growth:

Boundary Map: Identify areas where you need stronger boundaries to protect your soul—reducing social media time, saying no to overcommitment. Write an action plan for setting those boundaries.

Spiritual Growth Plan: If spirituality is a part of your soul-care, outline steps to deepen your connection such as meditation, prayer, or engaging with a spiritual community.

 ### *Something Extra Podcast*

- ► Tad Edwards, episode 115
- ► Lance Witt, episode 171
- ► Jillian Tedesco, episode 197

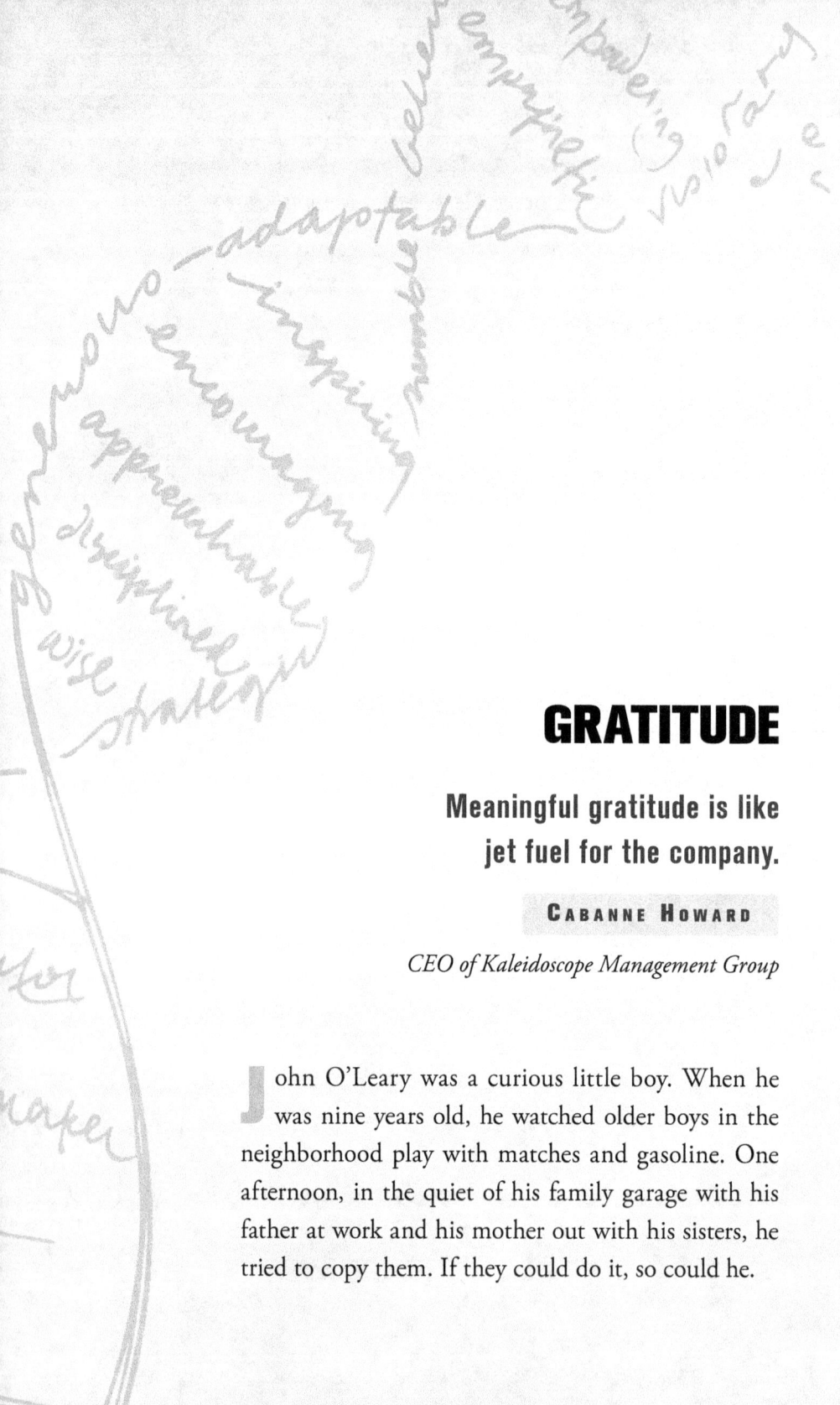

GRATITUDE

Meaningful gratitude is like jet fuel for the company.

CABANNE HOWARD

CEO of Kaleidoscope Management Group

John O'Leary was a curious little boy. When he was nine years old, he watched older boys in the neighborhood play with matches and gasoline. One afternoon, in the quiet of his family garage with his father at work and his mother out with his sisters, he tried to copy them. If they could do it, so could he.

His plans did not go as he expected. A fire exploded, consuming the garage, sending him flying 20 feet back against the garage wall and turning his whole world upside down. While sleeping in the basement, his older brother Jim heard the explosion and John's screams for help. Running into the front hall, he saw John engulfed in flames. Jim grabbed a rug and ran toward his brother, wrapping him up and carrying him outside. Jim rolled on top of John, burning himself in the process. He called 911 and made sure everyone was out of the house.

John woke up in a hospital bed where doctors had given him a 1 percent chance of living. He was burned on 100 percent of his body. He spent five months in the hospital, endured dozens of surgeries, and underwent years of physical therapy.

He lived.

He survived in no small part thanks to the efforts of others. Outside his immediate family, one of his first visitors at the hospital was Jack Buck, St. Louis's most iconic sports broadcaster and baseball Hall of Famer. Though John had never met Jack, he was well acquainted with Jack's voice, having fallen asleep many nights listening to baseball games on his portable radio after his parents had tucked him into bed.

The day Jack visited John in the hospital, a game-changing, years-long relationship began. John lay in the hospital bed unable to see, move, or talk, but he could hear.

"Wake up, kid. You are going to live. You're going to survive. We're going to have John O'Leary Day at the ballpark. We'll make it all worthwhile. Keep fighting."

Jack planted a seed of motivation in little John's mind—John O'Leary Day at the ballpark! During the five months John was in the hospital, Jack visited many times, each time offering the same incentive.

As John recovered, Jack challenged him to learn to write, which was no small task given that John's fingers had been amputated. He sent John a signed baseball with an attached note: "If you want another baseball, write a thank you letter."

In the following months and years, not only did John make it to the ballpark for multiple playoff games and World Series games, but he also received sixty baseballs—and learned to write in the process.

Today, John is a bestselling author, keynote speaker, and host of the popular podcast *Live Inspired*. His life story uniquely positions him to speak to others who are suffering or in crisis. And his advice might surprise you. He says one of the first steps toward resilience and grit is gratitude for what you have.

Gratitude.

He doesn't sugarcoat tragedy—his or anyone else's. It's okay to be sad, angry, and disappointed. He certainly has felt all those emotions and more. But when life seems to be falling apart around us, it's very easy to see *only* things that are out of place, bad, or wrong.

John combats that tendency every morning with a simple practice. He wakes up early, grabs a cup of coffee, goes outside, and looks to the east, waiting for the morning light to cut through the darkness. As he waits, he makes a list of things he's grateful for. Every morning he takes an inventory of what he has, not what he lacks. Sometimes he writes a gratitude list, and sometimes his gratitude is in the form of love letters to his family and friends.

Gratitude is a powerful motivator to keep going.

GIVE THANKS AND GIVE BACK

One of my favorite Bible passages is 1 Thessalonians 5:16–18, which says, "Rejoice always, pray continually, give thanks in all circumstances; for this is God's will for you in Christ Jesus." These verses remind us that gratitude is not about denying the challenges we face in life but about seeking out and acknowledging the silver linings, even in the midst of tough circumstances.

For the past five and a half years, our middle daughter, Paige, has been battling several autoimmune diseases that have completely derailed her plan to become a nurse. These illnesses have prevented her from pursuing the path she once envisioned and participating in many activities she would have otherwise enjoyed.

It has been hard—disappointing and discouraging in many ways. Yet amidst the difficulty, we've witnessed incredible silver linings. Paige's relationship with God has deepened profoundly as she's leaned on Him daily for strength, peace, purpose, and hope.

And her bond with Ally, our youngest daughter, has grown even closer. Together they discovered a shared passion for jewelry-making, which led to the launch of their business, Kindred Spirits Designs, on Black Friday of 2024. This beautiful venture has been a source of joy and purpose for both of them, a testament to finding light in the darkest seasons.

Gratitude teaches us to see beyond our pain and embrace the beauty that God is weaving into our stories, even when life doesn't go as planned. It reminds us that His plans are always greater than ours and that in all circumstances there is something to be thankful for.

Just as John O'Leary begins his day by practicing gratitude, our family, too, cultivates this mindset. For several years now, we have embraced a nightly tradition of gathering together to share what we are grateful for from the day. We take turns, going either from oldest to youngest or vice versa, with each person naming two or three things they're thankful for.

It's always uplifting—and often eye-opening—to hear each other's reflections. This practice not only fosters gratitude but also deepens our connection as a family. On many occasions, we've included Greg's mom, Dixie, who lives in another state, through FaceTime. Bringing her into this cherished tradition fills our hearts with joy and reminds us of the beauty of staying connected, even across the miles. This simple yet powerful habit has become a cornerstone of our lives, reminding us daily to look for the good and celebrate the blessings, big or small, that God places before us.

When I spoke to Jason Hall, former CEO of Greater St. Louis, about his career path and his work giving back to the local community, he also highlighted the importance of gratitude and family connections. He pointed to the sacrifices made by his parents and others who poured into him, allowing him to accomplish what he's done in his adult life. He reminds himself to not get too big for his britches. You don't always know what someone is up against, and it's important to thank family, friends, and other leaders in your life who have helped you get to where you are.

GRATITUDE IN THE MARKETPLACE

We often think of being grateful at the end of something. Only in looking back do we think about what we're thankful for. Marc Bernstein, founder and CEO of Balto, a platform that uses artificial intelligence to provide real-time guidance to contact center agents during customer calls, told me that his company values *begin* with gratitude.

Balto has only three stated values: Start with gratitude. Leadership is ownership. Always be growing. *Start with gratitude* means they approach all company success with a measure of humility. They are well aware that the contributions and efforts of others play a large role in their success. No one succeeds on their own. Marc acknowledges that sometimes you are just lucky, and being grateful allows you to be humble about how far you still have to go. Even as you strive for the next level, it's powerful to celebrate how far you've come and give thanks for all those who have contributed to your success.

I couldn't agree more. It's really hard to be disgruntled when you start with gratitude.

OPEN HANDS

John O'Leary considers himself extraordinarily ordinary. Even today, years after the tragic fire in his garage, he points with gratitude to the ordinary heroes who became his sources of strength. The first hero who showed up was his seventeen-year-old brother—not who John would have expected. As the months went on, that list of heroes grew. Firefighters, police officers, doctors, nurses, his family, Jack Buck, and several St. Louis Cardinals baseball players all made a difference in their own way. They showed up.

John says every leader needs to be grateful for who and what shows up. He acknowledges that we want to control what happens. We want to influence our teams and lead effectively—all important things. But he also says, "Can you imagine going through life with your hands completely open, just giving pure thanks for what you've got?"

Gratitude.

Reflection:

1. Who are the "ordinary heroes" in your life? How have their actions shaped who you are today? Reflect on the people who showed up for you in unexpected ways during challenging times. What lessons or values have you taken from their kindness and sacrifices?

2. How do you approach adversity in your life? Do you focus on what's missing or what remains? Consider a moment of significant loss or difficulty. What did you learn from that experience? How might gratitude have transformed the way you viewed the situation?

3. How does gratitude play a role in staying grounded? Reflect on moments when you felt deeply humbled by others' generosity or support. How do those moments influence your relationships and actions today?

4. In what ways do you express gratitude to others? How does that impact your relationships? Think about the people you interact with daily. Are there unspoken thank-yous you owe? How might expressing those thoughts change your connection with them? Showing gratitude with specificity is so powerful in the work setting. As leaders, we should notice the ways our team shows up well so we can call it out. Don't wait! The closer to the actual event that we can do this, the more powerful and meaningful it is.

5. If you were to live with "hands completely open," as John O'Leary suggests, what would that look like in your life? Reflect on areas where you are holding too tightly, whether in control, expectations, or fear. What could you gain by embracing a mindset of pure gratitude for what you have right now?

Action:

Gratitude Letters: Write a heartfelt thank-you note to someone who has made a difference in your life, much like Jack Buck inspired John O'Leary. This can be a powerful way to express your gratitude and honor their impact on your life. Not only does this simple act of acknowledgment uplift the recipient, but it also serves as a beautiful reminder to you of the profound difference that kindness and love can make. Take the time to celebrate your ordinary heroes and let them know just how extraordinary they are to you.

I personally did this with my parents individually before each of them passed away. I shared with them all the ways they had shaped my life and how much I cherished them. I have done this with my children and recently did an anniversary post to Greg on our fortieth anniversary, telling him all the things I love about him and what I appreciate the most. I believe it really touched him and will hopefully be something he reflects on often.

My good friend Dave Peacock, CEO of Advantage Solutions, shared with me that he wrote personal letters to each of his direct reports at Christmas, expressing what he appreciated about them. I'm sure those heartfelt notes are something his team will cherish for years to come.

Acts like these are more than just words; they are a way to pour life-giving encouragement into the people we care about.

Daily Gratitude List: Begin each morning with a list of things you're grateful for and meditate on them throughout the day as daily gratitude affirmations. Keep a journal and revisit it at the end of the week to see how it affects your mindset.

DAILY GRATITUDE

I woke up today.

I have loved ones.

I have food to eat.

I am still breathing.

I can move my body.

I have the ability to dream.

I have a place to call home.

I have someone who cares.

I have clean clothes to wear.

I can make choices for myself.

I am experiencing life on Earth.

I have the ability to grow each day.

Thank you for everything that I have and
for everything that is on its way to me.
There is so much to be thankful for.

Gratitude Walk: Take a mindful walk and focus on appreciating your surroundings. Journal about five things you noticed and felt grateful for during the walk.

 ## Connection:

Recognize the Unsung Heroes: Identify and thank someone in your workplace or community who doesn't always get recognized but plays a critical role in your life or work.

Gratitude as Leadership: Share with your team Marc Bernstein's principle, "Start with gratitude." Discuss how this mindset can shape company culture and relationships.

Paying It Forward: Volunteer as a family or team in your community. Reflect on how this act of service nurtures a sense of gratitude for what you have.

 ## Growth:

Gratitude in Leadership: Write an action plan for incorporating gratitude into your leadership or workplace practices. At Technology Partners, we use seed.hr as our recognition placeholder in our Slack channel. Teammates can call out one another with notes of gratitude, recognition, and oftentimes congratulations on hitting certain goals or milestones. But often it is used as a vehicle to thank a teammate and show gratitude publicly.

Gratitude Goals: Write down five ways you can practice gratitude more intentionally in your life. Make a plan to implement one each week for the next month.

Ally's Something Extra

Ally is truly one of the most grateful people I know. She finds joy in even the simplest moments, turning an ordinary day into something special. Whether it's a trip to Starbucks, a movie night, dinner out, or just spending time together at home, she never fails to express her gratitude.

Greg loves minestrone soup, so a couple years ago I decided to make a pot from scratch. As we sat around the table, I noticed Ally wasn't touching hers. Still, with her signature kindness, she looked at me and said, "Mom, thank you for the soup."

Paige, catching on, teased, "But you didn't like it!"

Without missing a beat, Ally matter of factly but ever so politely replied, "No, I don't!" as we all burst into laughter.

Even when something isn't quite to her liking, Ally's gratitude shines through. She has a way of appreciating the effort behind things, reminding us all to be thankful in every moment.

Something Extra Podcast

- ► Cabanne Howard, episode 59
- ► Jason Hall, episode 73
- ► John O'Leary, episode 94
- ► Marc Bernstein, episode 152
- ► Dave Peacock, episode 329

SELF-AWARENESS

The unexamined life is not worth living.

Greek philosopher

Cabanne Howard, founder of Kaleidoscope Management Group, has led a dynamic and adventurous life, marked by a series of global experiences followed by bold steps in her career. Her journey began during her college years when she studied abroad at the University of Lyon in France, which ignited her passion for international cultures and perspectives.

Cabanne's European adventure didn't end upon completion of her undergraduate degrees in art history and French. It marked the beginning of a career defined by exploration, innovation, and expertise in the field of communication. Inspired by her experiences, she made the bold decision to continue living abroad after graduation.

At the conclusion of Cabanne's time in Paris, a wonderful internship opportunity with Sotheby's International presented itself stateside. She enthusiastically accepted the position and put her art degree to work.

While the position with Sotheby's was an extraordinary way to jump-start her career, it wasn't long before Cabanne was swept up for a position in a prominent art gallery with locations in both St. Louis and New York. By all appearances, she was well on her way to a promising career in the art industry.

But then . . .

No one is buying million-dollar paintings, Cabanne thought to herself. This important observation marked the beginning of a significant period of introspection. "What I loved about the gallery was the business side of things—and I wasn't seeing a lot of business," commented Cabanne, "and I am way too talkative and extroverted for the gallery setting." Feeling like she was on the precipice of a major change, Cabanne began to ask herself hard questions.

> *What feedback have I received that I've ignored or dismissed? How do I handle failure? Do I have what it takes to actually do this and do it well? What feedback have my mentors given me that might help me right now?*

After considerable reflection and introspection, Cabanne made the boldest pivot of her life by taking a leap of faith into entrepreneurship. She founded Kaleidoscope Management Group where she now leads a thriving strategic marketing and communications services firm.

THE KEY TO EVOLVING LEADERSHIP

Success rarely follows a linear path, and Cabanne's journey is no exception. In fact, many of the most successful business leaders have nontraditional paths to achievement. Cabanne's unique ability to seamlessly blend creativity with analytical thinking—drawing on both her left- and right-brained strengths—has been a unique and significant asset in serving her clients and driving the firm's continued success over the years.

During an incredibly rich conversation, I asked Cabanne what she believes to be the something extra that every leader needs. "Self-awareness," she said.

The answer came quickly. As Cabanne progresses further in her career, she is sure her perspective on this question will continue to evolve, likely multiple times. But she's come to value self-awareness in a way she hadn't before. "There's often this notion that once you reach a certain level of seniority or leadership, you're expected to have all the answers, and your ideas are inherently sound," she explained. But the longer she continues, the more she realizes how important it is to pause, evaluate where her strengths lie, and recognize where she may have blind spots. There's tremendous power in this exercise.

Cabanne said, "It's incredibly impactful to acknowledge that reaching a leadership position doesn't mean you stop asking, 'What can I do better or differently today?' In fact, it's about constantly evolving and resisting the urge to settle into the mindset of *I've made it* or *I've figured it out.* The journey is ongoing, and that's a key focus for me right now. How do I seek out the blind spots so I can continue to grow, learn, and adapt rather than maintaining the status quo?"

THE TIMELESS POWER OF SELF-AWARENESS

Only by considering the definition of self-awareness can we fully appreciate how it has benefited scholars, business leaders, educators, entrepreneurs, and individuals across various fields throughout the years.

In its simplest terms, self-awareness is the ability to recognize and understand your own emotions, thoughts, behaviors, and their impact on others. It involves being conscious of your strengths, weaknesses, values, and motivations. Self-awareness allows individuals to reflect on their actions, make informed decisions, and manage their emotions effectively. It is a key component of emotional intelligence and plays an important role in personal growth, leadership, and building strong relationships. It forces us to find the blind spots that we all carry. There are places deep inside of us where we need to spend time in order to unearth the pieces of us that could be a hindrance to our success—both as individuals and as leaders.

This mindset of perpetual self-awareness and introspection isn't just a modern leadership principle; it echoes ancient wisdom. Socrates, for example, became synonymous with the concept of "know thyself" largely because of his emphasis on self-examination and the pursuit of wisdom through introspection. This phrase, which was inscribed at the Temple of Apollo at Delphi, reflects a central theme in Socratic philosophy—the belief that understanding yourself is essential to leading a virtuous and meaningful life.

By challenging individuals to understand their own motivations, limitations, and knowledge, Socrates made "know thyself" a cornerstone of his philosophy and the foundation of wisdom. This timeless principle resonates in modern leadership, as evidenced by the work of Rick Warren, founding pastor of Saddleback Church and author of *The Purpose Driven Life*; and Warren Buffett, CEO of Berkshire Hathaway.

Rick Warren emphasizes the importance of self-awareness in the context of spiritual growth and purpose. He believes that understanding yourself—your strengths, weaknesses, personality, and spiritual gifts—is crucial for living a purpose-driven life. In his book *The Purpose Driven Life*, he suggests that self-awareness helps individuals recognize how God uniquely designed them to fulfill a specific purpose.

Rick often speaks about how self-awareness leads to a more authentic and humble life, encouraging people to accept their God-given talents and limitations. He advises that knowing yourself allows you to serve others more effectively and align your life with God's plans rather than pursuing personal ambitions disconnected from your true self.

Self-awareness, in Rick's view, is closely tied to surrendering to God's will and seeking guidance from the Bible as it leads to greater clarity in your role and calling in life. "The way you see your life shapes your life. How you define life determines your destiny," he says.

Warren Buffet has often spoken about the importance of self-awareness in making wise investment decisions. Those decisions have landed him on the *Forbes* list of billionaires year after year. He emphasizes that knowing your strengths and limitations and having the humility to admit what you don't know is crucial for long-term success.

"You have to know yourself, and you have to know what you don't know," he says.

THE CRITICAL ROLE OF SELF-AWARENESS

A lack of self-awareness in the workplace can impact several key areas, including poor decision-making, an inability to identify team strengths and weaknesses, challenges in building trust and rapport, ineffective communication, and low emotional intelligence. These deficiencies can undermine individual and team performance, as well as overall organizational effectiveness.

Cabanne's journey exemplifies the power of self-awareness in leadership and the profound impact it has on both personal and professional growth. Her story is a testament to the importance of embracing introspection, constantly evolving, and remaining open to feedback as key elements of successful leadership.

Self-awareness is not just a trait to be developed but rather a foundational principle that empowers individuals to make informed decisions, foster collaboration, and navigate challenges with confidence. In a world that constantly demands adaptation and resilience, cultivating self-awareness remains one of the most effective ways to unlock leadership potential and drive lasting success.

Reflection:

1. What areas of your life or personality might you be overlooking? What recurring patterns in your life could reveal blind spots you haven't acknowledged?

2. How have you historically responded to constructive criticism?

3. What feedback have you consistently ignored or dismissed? Why might it feel uncomfortable to address?

4. How do your strengths empower you? How might your weaknesses hinder you in personal or professional growth?

5. If external expectations were removed, what would your most authentic self focus on? Why?

6. How can you ensure that you remain open to learning and evolving, even when you feel like you've achieved success?

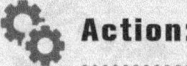 **Action:**

Strength and Weakness Map: Create a chart with two columns for your strengths and areas for improvement. Reflect weekly on ways you've leveraged strengths or worked on weaknesses.

STRENGTHS	AREAS FOR IMPROVEMENT

Decision : Reflect on a major decision you've made recently. Break it down into the emotions, thoughts, and feedback that influenced your choice.

DECISION	EMOTIONS	THOUGHTS	FEEDBACK
Ex:Taking a new position at work	Excitement, pride	This is a big step forward in my career	My spouse is concerned about the amount of travel that will be required

 **Connection:**

Friendly Coffee Chat: Share your reflections on blind spots and growth areas with a trusted friend or family member. Ask for honest feedback and make this a recurring chat for accountability.

Mentor Feedback: Actively seek a meeting with your boss or mentor in a professional setting, similar to what a quarterly or yearly evaluation would provide. But this time, you direct the areas on which you'd like feedback. Work together to make a growth plan for your career path.

Growth:

Daily Awareness Practice: Dedicate ten minutes at either the start or end of each day to reflect on your actions and their alignment with your goals and values.

Mindset Shift Exercise: Identify one limiting belief. Create an action plan to challenge it with evidence and positive behavior changes.

 Something Extra Podcast

► Cabanne Howard, episode 59

empowering

empathetic

calmness

adaptable

humble

inspiring

encouraging

approac

PART TWO

FOCUS ON OTHERS

GENEROSITY

You can have everything in life you want, if you will just help enough other people get what they want.

Z I G   Z I G L A R

Bestselling author and motivational speaker

John Ruhlin's life changed because of somebody he met during his sophomore year of high school. His girlfriend's dad, Paul, was an attorney known for his generosity. He would do radical things like hear about a deal on noodles and then proceed to put down thousands of dollars to buy every family in his church a year's supply.

If it wasn't noodles, it was something else. Paul was always making connections and helping others, showing generosity in some way. And it seemed to make a difference in his success. Even in financial dips and depressions, Paul continued to do well. As a young person, John Ruhlin observed and thought, "I want to be Paul when I'm sixty."

As a young adult, John took a job selling Cutco knives, what he calls the Rolex of cutlery. Naturally, one of the people he pitched was Paul. *Do you want to buy 100 pocket knives (at $80 each) for your best clients?*

Paul surprised him by refusing the pocket knives in favor of kitchen paring knives. John didn't understand. Why would he want to give a bunch of CEOs a kitchen tool? Paul explained, saying, "John, during forty years in business, I figured out that if you take care of the family and business, everything else takes care of itself."

Paul went on to explain that he didn't really care about the knives. He cared about the relationships with his clients—*and* their families. A generous gift that the whole family could use on a regular basis made an impact.

This was a lightning-bolt experience for John and a life-changing example of how generosity is a surefire way to build relationships. Though the girlfriend-boyfriend relationship did not last, John continued to sing Paul's praises and practice what he learned from him about generosity.

A CULTURE OF GIVING

Dr. Tom Hill exemplifies a life defined by generosity, intentionality, and a commitment to uplifting others. As an author, international speaker, entrepreneur, and CEO of Hill's Angels, Tom has consistently inspired those around him to live with purpose and extend kindness in extraordinary ways.

His philosophy on generosity is simple yet profound: Be committed to making a positive difference in every life you encounter.

One of his most memorable practices, which he models himself, is asking his clients to give a $100 bill every thirty days to a total stranger. This act, Tom emphasizes, is less about the amount and more about the heart behind it. It's a gesture that conveys care, hope, and the profound message that someone sees and values you.

Tom has countless stories of lives touched by these moments. He once gave to a Bosnian woman escaping an abusive relationship. He offered hope to a young soldier bidding farewell to his family at an airport before deployment. These small but powerful acts of kindness became the encouragement these individuals needed to keep moving forward.

Beyond his financial generosity, Tom has been widely celebrated for his willingness to give his time, wisdom, and unparalleled gift for connecting people. His legacy of generosity extends to countless individuals he has mentored, guided, and supported throughout his lifetime. Despite the onset of dementia, a poignant reminder of life's fragility, Tom's influence endures. This past year, I was deeply moved when I had the privilege of celebrating his eighty-ninth birthday. Amid his challenges, Tom recognized me—a moment that profoundly underscored the lasting impact of his relationships.

Tom's philosophy of generosity challenges us to ask this simple but profound question: *What do I have that I can share?* It's a question that shifts our perspective from scarcity to abundance and helps us see the resources, talents, and opportunities within us that can be used to bless others. While financial generosity is one way to make an impact, Tom reminds us that there are countless other ways to contribute. Perhaps it's a skill, a word of encouragement, or a connection that could help someone move closer to their goals and dreams, or lighten a burden they are carrying.

This mindset resonates deeply with me because making connections has been one of my personal superpowers. I find immense joy and fulfillment in knowing that a single introduction or relationship can unlock possibilities for someone else. Whether it's connecting a young professional to a mentor, introducing a business owner to a potential collaborator, or simply putting two like-minded individuals in a room together, I've seen time and again how these moments of intentionality can lead to transformative outcomes.

Connections are powerful because they reflect a belief in people and their potential. They say, "I see you. I believe in you. I want to help you succeed." And in a world where it's easy to feel isolated or overlooked, these gestures can be life-changing. Tom Hill exemplifies this kind of generosity, not only with his money but with his time and his uncanny ability to link people together in ways that inspire growth, opportunity, and impact.

One of the most profound aspects of this mindset is its accessibility. You don't need wealth, fame, or a title to be generous. Generosity flows from a heart that is willing to see others and act on their behalf. It's about choosing to live openhandedly, ready to give whatever you have to offer whether it's your resources, your talents, or your relationships.

Dr. Tom Hill's life serves as a powerful reminder that generosity at its core is about the heart. Unexpected kindness can change lives.

GENEROUS INVESTMENT

Life-changing generosity also comes in the form of mentorship. Dave Sanderson is a speaker, author, philanthropist, and authority on personal leadership. As a young person, his life was changed by a man named Bill.

Dave was working second and third shifts as the second assistant restaurant manager at Howard Johnson's. An older couple, Bill and his wife, Bonnie, came in regularly for coffee and ice cream and eventually struck up a friendship with Dave. Those nightly conversations turned into a years-long mentorship, with Bill introducing Dave to people and dropping mindset lessons on success.

In 1997, Bill presented Dave with two things: news that he was dying of lung cancer and a pile of handwritten notes. As it turned out, Bill had started collecting those notes back in 1929 when *his* mentor sat down with him and shared his hard-earned wisdom.

Bill's dying request was that Dave not let this wisdom die. Dave has honored that request by committing himself to leaving a legacy of lifting others up and sharing the wisdom that Bill gave him.

The Bible says, "A generous person will prosper; whoever refreshes others will be refreshed" (Proverbs 11:25). Generosity—whether it's in the form of finances, time, or mentoring—builds trust, loyalty, and morale in relationships and enhances collaboration, growth, and long-term success.

IT'S THE THOUGHTFUL THOUGHT THAT COUNTS

Inspired by his mentor's approach of giving generously without strings attached, John Ruhlin founded a business focused on gifting. His company helps others show generosity in a business setting. Giving more than is reasonable inspires loyalty, strengthens bonds, and helps leaders build communities where people naturally support and lift each other up.

Focusing on generosity is part of what John referred to as return on relationships (ROR) rather than just return on investment (ROI). He said that when you start to think creatively and show up for people differently than anybody else does, you will get different results.

It's not about spending more money, he said. It's about being more strategic, more creative, and more thoughtful. The gift is just a tangible reminder of the relationship.

Our family has received many, many generous, thoughtful gifts over the years, and we agree with John—the generosity that sparks the gift is what creates the emotional, meaningful connection. Sadly, John died unexpectedly in August 2024, leaving behind a wife and four young daughters, but his legacy of generosity lives on.

Reflection:

1. Think about your own definition of generosity. How would you define it? Compare it to examples from the stories in this chapter. Reflect on what generosity means in your life.

2. Recall a time someone was exceptionally generous to you. How did it make you feel? What impact did it have on your life? How did that moment shape your understanding of generosity?

3. Reflect on how you currently practice generosity. Is it financial, emotional, or time-based? Maybe you're noticing a lack of generous acts. What ways could you be more generous in your relationships or community?

4. Consider what holds you back from being generous. Is it fear of being taken advantage of, limited resources, or time constraints? How could these barriers be reframed?

5. Imagine what living a life marked by radical generosity would look like. What does that mean to you? How would it change your relationships, your community, and your sense of fulfillment?

 **Action:**

Generosity Journal: Keep a daily journal for a week. Write one generous act you witnessed or you personally performed each day. At the end of the week, reflect on its impact—on you, on your family, on strangers.

Personal Generosity Metrics: Create a chart to track your generosity over the next month. Record the date, the time, the resources, the opportunities you shared with others, and the overall impact.

Pay It Forward Project: Create a "Generosity Challenge" for yourself. Perform five unexpected acts of generosity for strangers over the next month (e.g., paying for someone's coffee or leaving a note of encouragement). Then reflect on how doing this anonymously made you feel. Did you enjoy being generous, even when not knowing for whom you did it and possibly not seeing the fruit of your labor?

Connection:

Community Outreach: Volunteer at a local shelter, food bank, or nonprofit organization as a group. Discuss how these experiences and programs shape your view of generosity.

Generosity Chain: Similar to the Pay It Forward project, start a "Generosity Chain" at your workplace or school. Give a small gift or favor to someone with the request that they pass it forward. Track how far the chain goes.

Giving Circle: Organize a small group of friends or family members to pool resources and decide together on a cause to support. Reflect on the collective power of generosity and its impact on others.

Family Generosity Plan: With your family or household, brainstorm ways to be generous together (e.g., volunteering, preparing care packages, hosting a community event). Model this for younger family members and learn from the wiser, older family members.

Growth:

Generosity Goals: Write down five ways you can incorporate generosity more intentionally into your life. Plan to implement one each week for the next month.

Generosity Legacy Statement: Write a personal mission statement about the role of generosity in your life. How do you want to be remembered for your acts of giving?

Something Extra Podcast

....

LOVE

Love is a verb.

GARY CHAPMAN

Author of The 5 Love Languages

im Bechtold was a senior executive at Procter & Gamble when he sat down with the chair of the P&G board, a man Jim considered to be one of the greatest leaders in the world. The subject of the conversation that day was Jim's PhD dissertation. Today was his opportunity to share what he'd learned.

At the time, P&G was rated the number-one company in the world for leadership, and Jim wanted to understand it at the DNA level. As part of his dissertation, Jim researched a number of other companies, and what he found was startling.

Seventy percent of the employees of all the companies he looked at did not trust their bosses or feel like their bosses cared about them. Employees said their bosses did not know their families or respect their family time and sent emails and texts on weekends, holidays, and vacations. Over and over, employees told Jim, "I'm just a cog in the wheel. No one really cares about me." They did not feel known or appreciated, and certainly not loved. They felt used.

The chair leaned forward, listening intently. "Jim, I don't even know how to think about this."

Jim replied, "This is the biggest opportunity for any CEO, any chair of the board I could ever speak to. Do *your* people care? Do they trust the people working for them?"

For Jim, the results of his research and his commitment to love as a leadership principle radically transformed how he treated his employees. Jim discovered that when employees feel genuinely valued, they are more likely to go above and beyond for the organization, even in difficult moments. Love transforms workplace cultures. It isn't just a "soft" principle but a strategic approach to building resilient, high-performing teams defined not by apathy or fear but by collaboration, trust, and mutual respect.

LEAD WITH LOVE

Love is not a word we often use in the workplace. Still, Marke Freeman, retired professional basketball player and president of

Max-OUT Foundation, says it's the *something extra* every leader needs. As Jim Bechtold discovered, Marke says simply caring about others and what is best for them makes all the difference. What are their needs? What are their goals and aspirations?

Specific actions that show your investment in others—that show love—are like deposits into a bank account. Marke says those deposits that come from a place of love, grace, and service will earn the trust and loyalty of your team. Leadership, after all, is not a dictatorship; at its core, leadership is service. And service based on love will make a powerful impression.

I couldn't agree more.

For as long as I can remember, I have chosen a word or phrase at the beginning of each year as that year's focus. In 2021, I chose *Love More*. I believe love is one of the most powerful keys in building strong relationships and lasting impact in the lives of others. Love, compassion, care, concern, and empathy for your people are important for every leader.

How do I show love, even in a business context? During my year of *Love More* and still today, I think about it in several areas.

- My words. Am I known for uplifting others through words of encouragement and support? Do I speak life to people?

- My presence. Do I exude calm, positivity, or joy when I walk into a room? Sometimes just being present with someone in their time of need is one of the most precious gifts I can give.

- My service. Am I the first to lend a hand when others need help? Acts of service—whether big or small—demonstrate a heart full of love.

> My compassion. Do others turn to me for understanding and empathy? My ability to listen and show genuine care can change someone's day or even their life.

LOVE WORKS

Joel Manby spent twenty years in the auto industry in management and marketing roles before becoming president, CEO, and director of SeaWorld and CEO of Herschend Enterprises, the largest family-owned theme park corporation in the United States. As a leader, he asked himself, *How would my leadership change if I let love guide every decision I make?*

After years of leading thousands of men and women, Joel is convinced that leading with love is incredibly effective. It's undeniable that love builds healthy relationships at home, so why not use the same behavior to build healthy relationships in a business environment? This perspective became Joel's North Star and transformed the culture of his organizations. He even wrote a book about it: *Love Works: Seven Timeless Principles for Effective Leaders.* Joel's book is a valuable resource that offers practical ways to bring love into a workplace culture. For Joel, love isn't just a feeling; it is an active commitment to treat others with care, respect, and selflessness.

When leaders practice love, they lay the groundwork for trust and loyalty, enabling their teams to flourish. Leading with love inspires others to take risks, innovate, and commit wholeheartedly to their work. Love is a transformational practice that enhances productivity, reduces stress, and builds resilience.

Joel says love is the only answer and the most important thing on earth that we do. In a world full of people who desperately want to be seen, known, and loved, leaders who lead with love can have a profound impact—not only on business results but in our country and world.

MORE THAN AN EMOTION

Gary Chapman, author of *The 5 Love Languages* that has sold over fourteen million copies and been translated into more than fifty languages, defines love as an attitude of genuine care for the well-being of others. Love, he explains, is an intentional mindset that says, "I'm here to enrich the lives of those I encounter," and it is expressed through purposeful actions that meet the emotional needs of others.

Love starts with empathy. Gary says a good leader has to develop the ability to ask questions of people and try to put himself in their shoes. When you listen long enough, you will be able to say, "That makes a lot of sense. I can see how you'd feel that way. If I was in your shoes, I'd probably feel exactly like you feel."

Empathy and understanding naturally lead to love, and the love languages framework can help leaders express that love in the way that's most meaningful to the other person. Acts of appreciation, words of affirmation, or taking time to understand a team member's needs are forms of love that build commitment. When leaders make the effort to understand their teams' unique motivations and challenges, they foster trust, loyalty, and deeper connections.

Let love guide your actions and watch as it builds stronger relationships, fosters resilience, and creates a lasting legacy.

Love isn't just an emotion. As Joel Manby says, it's the energy of life.

And, I would add, it's the energy of great leadership.

Reflection:

• •

1. Reflect on your career thus far. When have you ever felt truly cared for or valued in the workplace?

2. How do you currently show care and appreciation for the people you lead or work with? Are these actions meaningful to them? How could they be better aligned with their individual needs?

3. Think about how you've always viewed employee care. What biases might prevent you from expressing empathy and care in the workplace?

4. How do you balance the needs of the organization with the personal well-being of team members?

5. What specific steps have you taken to build trust with your team? How could you deepen that trust through intentional actions?

 **Action:**

....

Empathy Map Exercise: Create an empathy map for a team member or colleague that outlines their potential needs, challenges, and motivations. Also consider those who may be going through personal life events (e.g., birth of a child, a marriage, a diagnosis, an empty nest) that could use care. Use this to brainstorm ways to support them more effectively.

EMPLOYEE NAME	NEEDS	CHALLENGES	MOTIVATIONS	IDEAS FOR SUPPORT
Ex. John Smith	Extra help for latest assignment	Does not always get along with Suzy Q	Interested in a promotion this year because he is expecting his third child	One-on-one to talk about career aspirations Support for a plan during paternity leave

Acts of Appreciation Calendar: Dedicate one week to intentionally show appreciation to team members. Each day, express gratitude or recognition in a personalized way (e.g., verbal praise, a handwritten note, small tokens of appreciation).

STAFF APPRECIATION WEEK

We Are So Grateful For Wonderful Employees Like You!

May 1 — May 5

MON	TUE	WED	THU	FRI
NACHO AVERAGE EMPLOYEES! Join us for a Taco and Nacho Bar in the Staff Lounge! 11AM–1PM	**DONUT KNOW WHAT WE'D DO WITHOUT YOU!** Enjoy coffee and donuts in the breakroom 7–9AM	**BAR NONE, YOU'RE THE BEST!** Join us for a Fresh Salad and Soup Bar in the Staff Lounge 11:30AM–1:30PM	**YOU'RE THE SWEETEST!** Enjoy a candy buffet all day in the Staff Lounge!	**YOU HAVE A PIZZA OUR HEARTS!** Pizza party in the Staff Lounge with love

 **Connection:**

Pulse Check: Often when you meet with team members, it is to evaluate performance. Increase your connection by hosting one-on-one conversations as a pulse check. Ask open-ended questions to understand their goals, challenges, and needs. Use this insight to tailor your support for them. Or take a pulse check on your entire team. Jennifer Hopper, CIO of Save A Lot, holds a weekly "Ask Me Anything" meeting that allows her team to talk about whatever is on their minds.

Team Gratitude Board: Set up a physical or digital board where team members can write or post notes of appreciation for one another. Use this as a recurring reminder of the impact of small acts of love and care. At Technology Partners, this happens on a public Slack channel that everyone can see.

 ## Growth:

Leadership Cares Assessment: Create a survey for your team to evaluate how effectively you lead with love. Include questions about empathy, trust-building, and caring actions. Reflect on results and set goals for improvement.

Well-Being Workshop: Team-building events regularly focus on strengthening the team, increasing productivity, or unifying company vision and goals. Consider holding a well-being workshop where the focus is on team member rest, care, and personal goals. Some ideas are a nutritionist or sleep expert consult, a yoga retreat, or even a spa offering.

 ## Ally's Something Extra

When our kids were sixteen, fifteen, and fourteen, our family took a mission trip to El Salvador. We spent the first two days visiting two orphanages, and on the third day, we took our whole family into a prison filled with gang members. I'm referring to guys whose whole faces were nearly covered in ink, with teardrop tattoos signifying each person they had killed. I was starting to question our wisdom (or lack thereof) in putting our family in this situation.

We stood in the courtyard with a translator who was trying to help us connect with these guys. Unbeknownst to us, Ally walked away across the courtyard to the base of a wall where eight gang members were sitting and looking down at her. Before I could scream, "Ally, get back over here!" I noticed that Ally was just talking, her head moving back and forth, her hands animated. She was engrossed in a conversation. The guys didn't speak English, and she wasn't speaking Spanish, but they were all smiling from ear to ear. Ally didn't know that they were criminals. She didn't know they were supposed to be scary. All she knew was that they were people.

That day, she embraced the concept that *Imago Dei*—being made in the image of God—makes you worthy of attention and love. She saw the humanity of those men and engaged them with love and acceptance.

 Something Extra Podcast

- ► Marke Freeman, episode 81
- ► Dr. Gary Chapman, episode 140
- ► Jennifer Hopper, episode 164
- ► Jim Bechtold, episode 175
- ► Joel Manby, episode 234

VULNERABILITY

If you want to impress people, tell them about your successes. If you want to impact people, tell them about your mistakes.

Author, speaker, and leadership expert

For years, I thought leadership meant always having the right answers, being the one who knew the way forward, and being strong—without weakness. But life has a remarkable way of surprising us with its most profound lessons that change our perspective and how we navigate complexities. My biggest lesson came in the form of our daughter, Ally—Alexandra Alyse. It was a lesson wrapped in both excitement and fear.

When Ally was born with Down syndrome our world shifted in ways we never imagined. Overnight, we were thrust into a sea of unknowns, navigating waters we had never charted, and facing a future for which we weren't prepared. The sense of control and confidence we once had suddenly gave way to vulnerability—an unfamiliar, unsettling space.

Over time, though, Ally has taught us that vulnerability is not a weakness, but a powerful strength. Admitting that we don't have all the answers isn't a sign of failure—it's an invitation. It creates space for others to step in, share their insights, and collaborate in ways that enrich everyone involved. Vulnerability, I've come to realize, is a gesture of trust, a signal that you are willing to grow together with those around you.

THE POWER OF VULNERABILITY: BUILDING TRUST AND LOYALTY IN LEADERSHIP

Several years ago I had the pleasure of discussing this topic with a good friend of mine, Dr. John Townsend, a *New York Times* bestselling author, business consultant, leadership coach, and psychologist. During our conversation, we delved into the crucial role of vulnerability in leadership.

"The one thing I've found that's been the missing piece, the thing that makes all the difference, is leadership vulnerability," John explained. "When you can admit your mistakes and weaknesses with your people, you develop trust."

His words resonated deeply with me as they echoed the very lessons Ally had been teaching me all along. Vulnerability isn't just a personal strength; it's the key to cultivating trust and creating meaningful connections. It can feel counterintuitive, especially in a world that rewards confidence and decisiveness. But here's the paradox: *The more you lean into vulnerability, the more your leadership will resonate.*

John went on to say, "People identify and connect with you in these moments. This creates a culture of trust, which results in loyalty. Isn't that what every solid leader wants?"

When we consider the power of vulnerability, one thing we don't immediately think about is the way our vulnerability can affect other people. We know it fosters trust, builds rapport, creates meaningful connections, and has a host of other positive outcomes, but how about the idea that our stories can be powerful forces in the lives of other people?

Another guest of mine, Dr. Margie Warrell, former senior partner at Korn Ferry, bestselling author, keynote speaker, and leadership coach, touched on this. "I'm not perfect, and I'm still learning. Vulnerability allows us to connect meaningfully by showing that we struggle too. In a world that pressures us to seem like we have it all together, embracing our imperfections creates space for others to do the same. As I grow older and more comfortable with my humanity, I feel a responsibility to share my flaws because it helps others through their struggles. I believe that hiding our truths harms us, but being real opens the door to being a positive force in others' lives."

Recently I had a podcast conversation with Amanda McClerren, CIO and head of Digital Transformation at Bayer Crop Science. She told me that vulnerability is actually "top of mind" for her these days in her position of leadership.

"It's part of authenticity," she said. "It's how you show up in an authentic way. But I think it's a little deeper than that. I think it helps you. Vulnerability helps you get the help you need when you need it."

She went on to explain, "Reaching a certain level of leadership can unintentionally create barriers—whether it's the title in front of your name or the number of years you've been with the company. These things can create a distance. But by embracing a mindset of curiosity and openness, it breaks down those barriers. It unlocks something for you at work and, more importantly, within yourself. It reminds you that you don't have to know everything, and that's okay. It keeps you humble, curious, and eager to keep exploring and learning. It fuels your hunger to continue searching, growing, and evolving."

I wanted to know this: Has Amanda always been this way? Has she always possessed the ability to be vulnerable with her team?

"It is a skill I had to learn," she said. "I have not always been vulnerable, and frankly, while I am trying all the time, I don't think I am still that good at it. I had to experience some things in my personal life that were out of my control, that made me feel very uncomfortable. It's about the choices I made in those situations. Do you lean into it or do you fight it? I leaned in, and as a result, I became a better leader. I was able to connect to my team in a much deeper way."

EMBRACING VULNERABILITY AT EVERY RANK

Many of you may be navigating complex challenges in your leadership journey. You're managing teams, pursuing big opportunities, and even feeling the weight of needing to prove yourself. In the midst of these pressures, it's easy to fall into the trap of thinking that leadership means always having the answers or projecting unwavering confidence.

This belief in the power of vulnerability has been central to my leadership philosophy. But I didn't come to it naturally. Like many of you, I once believed that strength as a leader meant projecting confidence at all times, even when it was the last thing I felt.

Brené Brown, one of the most prominent thought leaders on the subject of vulnerability, defines vulnerability as "uncertainty, risk, and emotional exposure." She has spent years researching this complex subject in depth, interviewing people from all walks of life and spending time with high-powered executives, parents, teachers, scholars, army officials, and researchers in order to obtain the most comprehensive data.

During her time talking with and studying military leaders, a United States Army General told her, "We have to understand that vulnerability is not weakness; it's our greatest measure of courage." In an environment where strength is revered, expected, and ingrained in the culture, this statement was profound. It highlighted a shift in perspective, one that acknowledges the power of vulnerability even in settings where toughness is a core value. This recognition of vulnerability as courage challenged traditional views of leadership. It suggested that true strength isn't about invincibility but about the willingness to embrace uncertainty, admit imperfections, and connect on a deeper level with those you lead.

Vulnerability has emerged as one of the most powerful tools for leadership. It allows us to build deeper connections, foster trust, and create environments where innovation and collaboration can thrive. I've seen the power of vulnerability play out in mentoring relationships. It creates a bridge between mentors and mentees, breaking down hierarchical barriers and opening up real conversations.

At Technology Partners, we coordinate a popular leadership program called the Technology Leadership Experience. With TechLX, we have heard amazing stories from young leaders about how their mentor's willingness to admit they had once faced similar challenges—imposter syndrome, fear of failure—made them feel less alone. When you understand what your team needs on a human level, you unlock their potential.

When we as leaders have the courage to share our struggles, ask for help, and admit we don't have all the answers, we open doors for real connection and meaningful progress. It is how we build teams, organizations, and communities that not only succeed but thrive. True strength is found in our ability to be open, honest, and human with those we lead.

Through my own journey with Ally and in my leadership experience at Technology Partners, I've come to realize that vulnerability is one of the greatest strengths a leader can embody. Ally has taught me more about vulnerability than any seminar, mentor, or leadership program ever could. It's not about having all the answers; it's about creating space for others to step in, share insights, and grow together. Vulnerability builds trust, fosters resilience, and opens the door for deeper connections, whether in the workplace or at home.

When you lead with vulnerability, you don't just become a better leader; you become a better human being.

Reflection:

....

1. How did your upbringing shape your understanding of vulnerability?
    Were you taught that showing emotions was a strength or a weakness?

2. How do you personally define vulnerability? In what areas of your
    life do you resist being vulnerable?

3. What barriers (emotional, social, professional) prevent people from embracing vulnerability? Do any of those barriers resonate with you?

4. How do you respond to the vulnerability of others? Are you someone who encourages openness, or do you struggle with discomfort when others share openly?

5. How do you think vulnerability influences the way you lead or interact with others in your personal and professional life?

 **Action:**

Vulnerability Map: Fill in this diagram as you reflect on your layers of vulnerability. What areas can move toward the center?

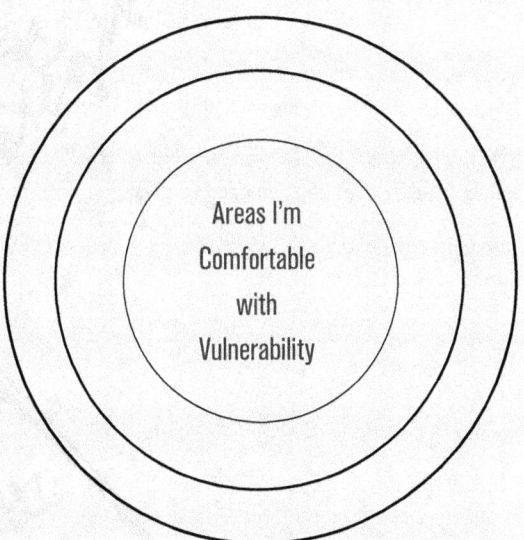

Areas I'm
Comfortable
with
Vulnerability

Vulnerability Tracker: Fill out this daily chart to document small moments of vulnerability each day.

YOUR VULNERABLE ACT (What You Shared or Risked)	HOW IT FELT IN THE MOMENT	WHAT THE OUTCOME WAS	WHAT YOU LEARNED

Connection:

The Go First Challenge: In a conversation with a friend, colleague, or family member, practice initiating vulnerability. Share a personal struggle, lesson, or moment of uncertainty, and observe how it shifts the dynamic.

Ask for Help Experiment: Choose one small but meaningful thing you need help with (work, emotional support, advice). Ask someone for help and notice how it feels to let someone support you.

Growth:

Thirty-Day Comfort Zone Stretch: List five vulnerable actions you normally avoid (e.g., apologizing first, speaking up in a meeting, sharing your real emotions). Commit to one action per week for the next month to practice getting out of your comfort zone and into your vulnerable zone.

VULNERABLE ACTION I TYPICALLY AVOID	WEEK 1 ACTION	WEEK 2 ACTION	WEEK 3 ACTION	WEEK 4 ACTION
Ex. Share my opinions during staff meetings	*Intentionally assess when I should speak up*	*Respond to a coworker's ideas during a meeting*	*Write out a script of my ideas*	*Share my thoughts unprompted during a meeting*

Something Extra Podcast

► Dr. John Townsend, episode 12
► Amanda McClerren, episode 320
► Dr. Margie Warrell, episodes 219 & 325

RELATIONSHIPS

If you want to go fast, go alone. If you want to go far, go together.

AFRICAN PROVERB

Food was hard to come by in Orv Kimbrough's childhood home. So when he woke up hungry one morning and found only a box of crackers in the kitchen, he knew he needed to ask his mother before he ate them. She was asleep in the other room, so he tiptoed in carefully.

"Mom? Mom, can I . . ."

No response.

Eight-year-old Orv lightly touched his mother's shoulder and then began to shake her.

Still no response.

When the paramedics arrived, they pronounced her dead. That terrible day marked the beginning of Orv's journey in the foster care system, a journey marked by instability, loss, and separation from his siblings.

Unlike many children, Orv had no long-term parental figures to guide him. Instead, he relied on relationships that came into his life at critical moments—mentors, teachers, counselors, and community members who spoke words of life and encouragement when he had no vision for himself.

One of those pivotal moments came in eighth grade. Orv was the class clown, often disruptive and unfocused. One day, his math teacher hugged him and said something that Orv never forgot: "I love you." Later, a counselor echoed those same words: "Your life has value and purpose, and I love you."

Those relationships, as well as those with members of the parish he attended as a young boy and foster families he lived with, gave Orv the belief in himself he needed to push forward. Orv grew up with many deficits, but as he got older, he began to be empowered to shape his environment rather than simply be shaped by it. He began to focus on building relationships that created a context for higher performance. Put simply, he surrounded himself with good people.

Faith, mentorship, and relationships shaped Orv's entire career trajectory and the full and purposeful life he now leads. Today, as a CEO, Orv reflects on the truth he sees displayed in his life story, that every breakthrough is on the other side of the right relationship.

Whether in business, leadership, or life, relationships are the greatest currency. They shape who we become, open doors we never imagined, and sustain us through our hardest moments.

RELATIONSHIPS FOR LIFE

I think of relationships like concentric circles, with God at the center. My relationship with God is where it all starts. By prioritizing this vertical relationship first, my ability to pour into others is multiplied exponentially. It is the foundation that gives me the strength, wisdom, and capacity to reach out horizontally and build deeper, more meaningful connections with others.

The next circle includes my husband and children, followed by extended family, close friends, colleagues, and the broader community. This framework helps me keep my priorities in order because while I am deeply energized by people both personally and professionally, I must be intentional about where I invest my best energy. I never want to give the best of myself to others while leaving only the breadcrumbs for God and my family. The order matters.

The opportunity to positively impact someone's life is what keeps me going, even in the toughest times. I've known many people who, by the world's standards, may not have much, yet they are among the richest individuals I know because of the deep, meaningful relationships they've cultivated over the years. As Tony Robbins says, "The richness of your life is directly related to the quality of your relationships." I wholeheartedly believe this, and I've found that some of my greatest moments of growth have come through the people around me.

John Maxwell speaks extensively about the power of relationships and their profound impact on personal growth. John is one of the most sought-after leadership voices of our time, yet he remains intentional about continuously building stronger relationships. Each quarter he schedules what he calls a Learning Lunch. He invites someone "bigger" and "better" to lunch with the sole purpose of learning from them. He comes prepared with a series of thoughtful questions such as "What are your greatest learnings from failure?" This kind of intentional relationship-building is something I deeply admire.

Healthy relationships are a delicate balance of give and take. When this balance is off, relationships can become strained, one-sided, or even transactional. True, life-giving relationships require mutual investment, genuine care, and a commitment to growth—not just for ourselves but for those we are privileged to journey alongside.

These are some things I like to keep in mind as I intentionally nurture the relationships in my life. Maybe they'll help you too.

> **Leverage your network.** Don't underestimate the power of your connections. Whether you know someone with expertise or a resource someone else needs, make those introductions. You have more power than you think to open doors for others.

> **Celebrate others' wins.** Be intentional about recognizing and celebrating the successes of people around you, no matter how big or small. A simple acknowledgment can fuel further growth and foster stronger relationships.

> **Create opportunities for growth.** If someone is ready to take the next step but doesn't know how, help them identify or create growth opportunities. Whether it's a new connection, a course, or a resource, you can be the catalyst for their success.

▶ **Be present and listen.** In every conversation, truly listen to what others are saying. Often, just being fully present gives people the confidence to share their needs, and your attention can be the spark that propels them forward.

FULL-CIRCLE CONNECTIONS

When Dena Ladd was the executive director of Missouri Cures, a nonprofit whose mission is to promote and protect medical research in the state of Missouri, she spent years advocating for medical research by building strong relationships with scientists, policymakers, and patient advocates. Dena has since gone on to other consulting ventures, but her work at Missouri Cures was impactful because of her ability to bring people together. Through initiatives like the WISE (Women in Science & Entrepreneurship) Conference, she connected female scientists, engineers, and business leaders, helping them build relationships that accelerated careers, drove innovation, and broke barriers in male-dominated industries.

One moment stands out to her as a reminder of how interconnected leadership relationships can be. At a networking event, she was introduced to a tech entrepreneur. As they talked, Dena realized something surprising. This person's mother had been a key volunteer in one of Dena's early political campaigns years ago. What seemed like a random introduction was actually a full-circle moment, proving that the connections we build today often shape our future success in ways we don't anticipate.

That moment reinforced what Dena has experienced time and time again. Leadership isn't just about expertise or hard work; it's about the relationships you cultivate along the way. When leaders understand the power of building and maintaining strong networks, they create a ripple effect of success for themselves and for those around them.

In fact, Dena told me she thinks the *something extra* every leader needs is networking and communication skills, which can be summed up as the ability to form relationships. Dena didn't grow up in St. Louis, but after twenty years, she's very connected. She jumps on opportunities to attend events and meet new people, viewing those new relationships as an investment, not a transaction.

Too often, people approach networking and leadership relationships with a transactional mindset, seeking connections only when they need something. But true leaders invest in relationships long before they need them. Dena's success in medical research advocacy was built on this principle. She collaborated with top-tier institutions, and her relationships extended beyond professional necessity. She believes in deep, authentic connections that foster long-term collaboration and trust. Strong relationships are built over time, and investing in people—mentoring, supporting, and staying connected—leads to greater opportunities down the road. The most impactful leaders don't just focus on what someone can do for them today; they cultivate relationships with an eye toward the future.

At its core, leadership isn't about authority or expertise; it's about people. The strongest leaders invest in relationships, open doors for others, and nurture connections with intentionality.

Reflection:

1. Who are the key relationships that have shaped your life? How did those people impact your personal or professional growth?

2. Have you ever had a breakthrough that was made possible because of a relationship? How did that connection change your trajectory?

3. How intentional are you in building and maintaining relationships, not just for personal gain but for mutual growth and support?

4. In what ways do you invest in others—mentoring, supporting, or opening doors for them—without expecting anything in return?

5. What steps can you take to shift from a transactional mindset in relationships to a long-term investment approach where trust and collaboration grow over time?

 **Action:**

Personal Relationship Scorecard: Rank yourself on these relationship factors. What areas do you need to improve?

1. **Trust and Reliability:** How dependable and trustworthy am I in my relationships?

    1 • I struggle with keeping commitments or being reliable.
    2 • I try to be trustworthy but sometimes fall short.
    3 • I am generally reliable, but I could improve in some areas.
    4 • People can count on me, and I follow through consistently.
    5 • I am a rock for others; they trust me deeply and without hesitation.

2. **Communication and Listening:** How well do I communicate and listen in relationships?

   1 • I often interrupt, misunderstand, or struggle with open communication.
   2 • I communicate, but I don't always listen or express myself effectively.
   3 • I am a decent communicator but could improve in depth and consistency.
   4 • I actively listen, engage in meaningful conversations, and communicate well.
   5 • I am an excellent communicator, both expressing and receiving thoughts clearly.

3. **Support and Encouragement:** How well do I show up for others emotionally and practically?

   1 • I rarely offer support, or I tend to prioritize my own needs.
   2 • I help when convenient, but I don't always make an effort.
   3 • I try to be supportive but sometimes struggle with consistency.
   4 • I regularly support and encourage the people in my life.
   5 • I am a strong source of encouragement and always make time for others.

4. **Conflict Resolution and Boundaries:** How well do I handle disagreements and set healthy boundaries?

   1 • I avoid conflict or react poorly, and I struggle with setting boundaries.
   2 • I try to manage conflict, but I often feel uncomfortable or defensive.
   3 • I handle conflict fairly well but could improve in certain situations.
   4 • I navigate disagreements with maturity and respect personal boundaries.
   5 • I resolve conflicts constructively and set healthy boundaries with ease.

5. **Investment and Reciprocity:** How much effort do I put into maintaining and deepening relationships?

   1 • I rarely put in effort unless I need something.
   2 • I try to invest, but I often get distracted or don't follow up.
   3 • I maintain relationships, but I could be more intentional.
   4 • I prioritize and nurture relationships with consistent effort.
   5 • I actively cultivate and deepen relationships, always looking for ways to give.

 **Connection:**

Reverse Networking List: Let's think intentionally about your relationships and how you can serve others. Instead of listing people who could help you, list people you can help. Plan to support them, whether through mentorship, introductions, or resources.

Relationship : List the key relationships in your life (personal, professional, community). Identify which ones need more intentional investment and create a plan to nurture them.

Name of Relationship	Check If Personal Relationship	Check If Professional Relationship	Does This Relationship Need More Investment at This Time?	What Is Your Plan to Invest in This Relationship?
Ex. Sister who just moved into town	X		Yes. She is new to the city and needs resources and support.	I plan to help her move into her new apartment and introduce her to some of my network.

 **Growth:**

Apologize and Restore a Relationship: Think of a relationship that has been damaged or neglected. Take a step toward reconciliation by offering an apology, expressing gratitude, or reestablishing contact.

Set Boundaries Where Needed: Growth in relationships isn't just about giving. It's also about setting healthy boundaries. Identify a relationship where you need to set clearer expectations and take action.

Reflect on the Energy Exchange in Relationships: Make a list of people who uplift you and those who drain you. How can you spend more time with the former and set boundaries with the latter?

 Something Extra Podcast

- ► Dena Ladd, episode 20
- ► Orv Kimbrough, episode 23

SACRIFICE

Life's most persistent and urgent question is, "What are you doing for others?"

MARTIN LUTHER KING, JR.

Minister and civil rights activist

ark Whitacre was a rising executive at Archer Daniels Midland (ADM), an American multinational food processing and commodities trading corporation, when he found himself at a moral crossroads.

Mark had amassed great material wealth, widespread notoriety as one of the youngest executives in the company's history, and all the perks that came with his position. However, when his wife, Ginger, discovered the price-fixing scheme Mark was involved in and realized that everyday consumers were the ones being harmed, she made a bold and selfless decision. She told Mark that either he would report the scheme to the FBI or she would.

Her courage was remarkable, especially given the uncertainty of what would happen to Mark as a result. She risked their comfort, security, and his entire career for the sake of integrity and justice. In that moment, Ginger exemplified true sacrifice, choosing to stand for what was right no matter the cost.

Mark also leaned into the sacrifice, becoming an FBI informant and wearing a wire for three years to expose corruption in his own company. The personal consequences were devastating. Wearing the wire was risky. He was told, "Mark, if these guys catch you, they're going to kill you." He was under extreme stress. He slept only two or three hours a night. He lost 60 pounds, leading people in his company to wonder if he had cancer. He was on the verge of a nervous breakdown.

Unfortunately, Mark ended up losing his career, reputation, and ultimately his freedom when he was required to serve over eight years in prison for his financial misconduct during the time he was an FBI informant.

While in prison, Mark experienced a life-changing spiritual awakening when he became a Christian through the influence of Chuck Colson, an attorney and political advisor to President Richard Nixon. Chuck had served time in prison for his role in the Watergate scandal.

That defining experience enhanced Mark's commitment to personal sacrifice on behalf of the greater good.

FOR THE SAKE OF OTHERS

For those in leadership roles—whether in business, community work, or personal life—doing the right thing is rarely easy. Leaders must be willing to pay the price for ethical decision-making, even when it leads to loss in the short term.

Randy Gravitt, cofounder along with Mark Miller of Lead Every Day, talks about the baseball strategy called bunting. In baseball, bunting provides the perfect metaphor for sacrificing for the greater good. When a player lays down a bunt, they are often giving up their own chance to get on base or hit a big play to advance a teammate into a better scoring position. This selfless act prioritizes the success of the team over individual achievement.

Similarly, in leadership, teamwork, and life, true success often comes from acts of sacrifice—choosing what benefits the greater good rather than seeking personal glory. Just as a batter may sacrifice their at-bat to move a runner closer to home, individuals in organizations, families, and communities may set aside personal recognition, comfort, or ambition to support a larger mission or shared goal.

In essence, bunting is a tangible reminder that sometimes the most impactful contributions aren't the flashy, headline-grabbing moments but the small, intentional sacrifices that set others up for success. Albert Einstein said, "Only a life lived for others is a life worthwhile."

When I think of sacrifice, I think of my husband, Greg. He rarely thinks about himself. He has always worked long, hard hours—not for personal gain or to build a reputation as a brilliant businessman but for something far greater. Notoriety and ego have never mattered to him, and that is one of his many qualities I deeply love and admire.

From the time we were in high school, Greg has been driven by a desire to make the world a better place, often for people he has never even met. When we dreamed together as a young couple, the vision was always the same: If we can build a company that does well, we can do more good in the world. That belief has guided Greg every step of the way. In pursuing it, he has made countless sacrifices, not for himself but for the sake of others.

SACRIFICE IS A DAILY CHOICE

Lucas Rouggly's journey also exemplifies sacrifice—lived out daily. As the founder and executive director of LOVEtheLOU, a nonprofit dedicated to revitalizing North St. Louis, Lucas made the radical choice to move his family into one of the city's most challenged neighborhoods. Instead of offering aid from a distance, he and his family immersed themselves in the community, experiencing the same struggles as those they sought to serve. Lucas's leadership is deeply rooted in the idea that love requires sacrifice—not just financial giving but the surrender of personal ambitions, comfort, and even control.

"When you truly love, you're laying down your life," he said. "You're laying down your vision, your kingdom."

He let go of personal control over his organization, allowing community members—the very people he had come to serve—to take on leadership roles. By elevating their voices instead of asserting his own, he empowered the community in ways that traditional leadership models often fail to achieve.

One of the most moving stories from LOVEtheLOU is that of a young man named Jamel. He grew up walking miles to attend church in North St. Louis. Over the years, Jamel found mentorship, family, and hope through LOVEtheLOU. When Lucas asked him what had made the biggest difference in his life, Jamel didn't mention financial aid or programs. Instead, he pointed to a simple meal shared with the Rouggly family—an act of inclusion and belonging that reshaped his vision for his future.

Lucas's story challenges conventional leadership wisdom. Leadership is not about holding on to power but about relinquishing it for the good of others. Sacrifice in leadership means stepping aside, making room, and allowing others to rise.

Lucas's leadership is a powerful example of relational investment, servant leadership, and personal sacrifice. His approach challenges the idea that leadership is about power or position. It's about proximity, presence, and putting others first.

Both Mark Whitacre and Lucas embody this principle in different ways—one through moral courage and the willingness to risk everything for truth and the other through daily, lived-out humility in service to others. Mark's sacrifice exposed corruption and helped reform a corrupt system. Lucas's sacrifice has built a thriving community. Both show that when leaders embrace sacrifice, they make a profound impact and create lasting change.

Sacrifice is a concept that resonates deeply across all aspects of life, from personal growth to leadership and service. It is the willingness to give up something valuable—comfort, security, ambition, or even reputation—for the sake of a greater cause. True leadership is often defined not by achievements alone but by the sacrifices made along the way.

Reflection:

....

1. Have you ever faced a moment where doing the right thing required personal loss? What factors influenced your decision? Would you make the same choice today?

2. Think back to a time when someone else's sacrifice significantly impacted your life. How did their actions influence your own leadership values and decisions?

3. In what ways has leadership forced you to surrender personal ambitions? How did that impact your sense of purpose?

4. If you knew that a major sacrifice today would create lasting change for others, what would hold you back from making it?

5. If someone were to reflect on your leadership years from now, what sacrifices would you want them to remember? How can you begin living that legacy today?

 **Action:**
···

Sacrifice Inventory: Make a list of your roles and responsibilities and identify where sacrifice may be required. Note areas where personal comfort, ambition, or resources could be surrendered for a greater impact.

LIST OF ROLES AND RESPONSIBILITIES	HOW TO SACRIFICE IN THAT TASK
Ex. I'm a team leader.	*I can sacrifice my time to mentor each member of my team for one hour a week.*

Develop a "Less of Me, More of Others" Habit: Identify one daily action (letting others speak first in meetings, choosing service over convenience, sharing credit) that reinforces sacrificial leadership. Write out your first log here by sharing what your daily action was and how it reinforced your act of sacrifice.

Date:

Action:

How this action was a sacrifice:

 **Connection:**

Recognition of Others' Sacrifices: Take time to acknowledge and thank people in your personal or professional life who have made sacrifices for you. Express gratitude in a meaningful way.

Sacrificial Listening: For one week, commit to prioritizing others' needs in conversations. Focus on listening without immediately offering solutions or asserting your own agenda.

Growth:

Daily Reflection Practice: End each day by asking, "How did I put others before myself today? What sacrifices did I make for a greater purpose?" Adjust your actions based on what you learn.

Leadership Challenge Commitment: Set a short-term challenge (seven-day, thirty-day) where you intentionally practice selfless leadership in different areas of your life. Document your experiences.

Comfort Zone Challenge: Choose one area in your life where you typically avoid sacrifice (taking risks, having difficult conversations, prioritizing others). Challenge yourself to act differently.

 Something Extra Podcast

- ► Mark Whitacre, episode 117
- ► Lucas Rouggly, episode 248
- ► Randy Gravitt, episode 316

COMMUNICATION

The single biggest problem in communication is the illusion that it has taken place.

GEORGE BERNARD SHAW

Playwright and critic

August 29, 2005—many can recall where they were as they nervously watched Hurricane Katrina make landfall on the Gulf Coast of the United States, leaving a trail of destruction that would become one of the deadliest natural disasters in American history.

Entire neighborhoods were swallowed by floodwaters, homes were reduced to splinters, and thousands of desperate residents were left stranded on rooftops, pleading for rescue.

But beyond the raw power of the storm, another force contributed to the disaster's devastation—one that didn't come from nature but from within the halls of government itself. It was *a catastrophic failure of communication.*

The first cracks in the response to Hurricane Katrina emerged even before the storm hit. Meteorologists and emergency management officials issued grave warnings about the storm's potential for destruction, particularly in New Orleans. Days before landfall, the National Hurricane Center predicted with eerie accuracy that Katrina's storm surge could overtop levees, causing *catastrophic* flooding. Despite these dire forecasts, government officials at all levels failed to communicate the urgency of the situation in a way that mobilized an effective response.

As the levees broke and water surged through the streets of New Orleans, communication failures became even more pronounced. Residents who had not evacuated sought shelter in the Superdome and the Convention Center, believing they would be safe. But as conditions deteriorated inside—food and water ran out, sanitation collapsed, and violence erupted—government officials seemed either unaware or unable to coordinate a response.

As the days dragged on, our nation watched in horror. The Superdome and Convention Center became symbols of government failure with thousands enduring inhumane conditions while relief efforts remained paralyzed by indecision and miscommunication.

By the time a robust federal response finally arrived, it was too late for many. More than 1,800 lives were lost, and tens of thousands of survivors were left traumatized. The government's failure to communicate effectively during Katrina shattered public confidence in disaster preparedness and response.

In the years since Katrina, emergency management strategies have evolved, with greater emphasis on clear communication, coordinated response systems, and streamlined decision-making. Yet the disaster remains a stark reminder of what happens when leaders fail to communicate in times of crisis.

Words—spoken or left unsaid—can mean the difference between life and death.

HOW TO COMMUNICATE LIKE A GREAT LEADER

While the consequences of poor communication in business may not be a life-or-death situation, the principles remain the same. Clarity, alignment, and trust are non-negotiable. Without communication, progress stalls. Whether leading a company or a country, managing a team, or navigating daily interpersonal interactions, the ability to connect, align, and inspire through words is what separates great communicators—whether government or civilian—from the rest.

How often do we say something, believing we've made our point clear only to realize later that it was misunderstood? Or conversely, how often do we hear something but interpret it in a way that wasn't intended? These breakdowns in understanding don't happen because of a lack of communication; they happen due to ineffective communication.

Jeremie Kubicek and Steve Cockram, authors of *The Communication Code*, explain it this way: "Communication is the key to relational trust. Just because an email or text has been sent doesn't mean communication has actually happened—that's merely transmission."

Bill Ellis, one of my podcast guests and host of his own podcast, *What's The Point*, said, "For years, I've heard companies and individuals emphasize the need for more communication. But I call that out for what it is—*nonsense.* We don't need more communication; we need more *effective* communication. There's a critical difference."

Being an effective communicator is not just about speaking clearly. It's about fostering meaningful dialogue, listening actively, and creating an environment where ideas can be shared openly. Communication is a skill that requires constant refinement as it plays a critical role in leadership, collaboration, and problem-solving. One of the most powerful ways to enhance communication is by asking better questions.

Another guest, Bob Tiede, in the book he co-authored with Michael J. Marquardt, *Leading with Questions*, emphasizes that great leaders don't just provide answers; they ask the right questions. In fact, Bob refers to himself as a recovering "tellaholic." I bet several of us can relate both in our workplaces and our families. We should refrain from telling others our opinions or solutions and instead *lead* them by asking thoughtful, well-placed questions.

Great questions invite engagement, spark curiosity, and empower others to contribute their insights. When leaders shift from a telling mindset to an *asking* mindset, they foster deeper connections, unlock creativity, and create a culture of trust. Instead of assuming they have all the answers, they become facilitators of discovery, allowing their teams to feel valued and heard.

Effective communication is not just about transmitting information; it's about understanding, learning, and growing together. By leading with questions, leaders not only gain better insights but also encourage their teams to think critically, problem-solve, and take ownership of their ideas. In a world that is constantly evolving, the ability to communicate effectively through curiosity and active listening is what sets exceptional leaders apart.

Effective communication depends on understanding *how* people process information. People process information differently. Some need direct and concise messaging, while others require more context and detail. Some prefer written communication, while others engage better through verbal discussion. Recognizing these nuances and adapting to them are the difference between simply *saying* something and truly *communicating* it.

THE POWER OF WORDS

Jason Weems grew up in a small town an hour south of St. Louis where he enjoyed the close-knit community of his childhood. While he wasn't always certain about his career path, a passionate teacher often spoke to Jason about the world of computers, introducing him to their seemingly unlimited potential. These conversations sparked a keen interest that led Jason to pursue IT. After earning his MBA from St. Louis University, Jason built an impressive career with IT leadership roles at Express Scripts and Cigna before joining Soleo Health where communication is at the core of his leadership strategy.

"This notion that words matter becomes really important," Jason shared with me. "Understanding your audience and what they need—and reading your audience—is a skill set."

Like many leaders, Jason initially believed that delivering a message was enough—that if he spoke clearly, his audience would automatically understand. Over time, he learned that true communication is not about broadcasting information but ensuring alignment. His approach focuses on understanding the needs of business partners, teams, and executives, and then tailoring his message to create clarity and shared objectives.

In today's fast-paced business environment where we are constantly bombarded with messages, clarity and intentionality matter more than ever. Leaders who are intentional about their communication—unlike the leadership during the Hurricane Katrina debacle—don't just convey information; they inspire action, align teams, create connection, and drive meaningful results.

When we take a look at effective workplace communication, we realize it is more than just exchanging information. It's about aligning teams, building trust, and driving success. Studies show that the average professional encounters thousands of messages daily—DMs, emails, meetings, texts, and social media notifications. With this overwhelming volume, the ability to communicate with clarity and impact is a necessity in effective communication.

Communication has always been and likely always will be the foundation of human progress. Early civilizations relied on it for survival, whether through hieroglyphic storytelling or written records. Today, communication remains just as critical, shaping everything from relationships and consumerism to leadership effectiveness and company culture.

Personally, this is something I need to work on constantly. It is not a skill we are automatically born with, but it is a skill that, with practice, can be refined and matured over time. For me, embracing Bob Tiede's leading with questions approach has been a game-changer. Instead of feeling the need to have all the answers, I've learned that the right question at the right time can unlock deeper conversations, foster collaboration, and inspire new ideas. When leaders communicate in a way that values inquiry over instruction, they create an environment where innovation thrives and people feel heard, respected, and empowered.

In the end, effective communication isn't just a leadership tool. It's a lifelong discipline that strengthens relationships, builds trust, and fuels both personal and organizational growth. And the best part? It's a skill we can all continue to develop, one question at a time.

Reflection:

....

1. Recall a time when communication—or its absence—significantly affected your understanding of a situation or a relationship. What did you learn from it?

2. Have you ever seen someone's communication completely transform a situation or align a group? What made it so effective?

3. What is your focus when speaking? Is it what you want to say or what the other person needs to hear? What's more important?

4. Do you adapt your communication style to different audiences? What challenges do you face in doing so?

5. Do you seek feedback on how well your messages are understood? If so, what does that feedback reveal about your communication strengths and weaknesses?

 **Action:**

Listening : For a day, track how often you listen without interrupting versus when you respond quickly, noting the impact on your interactions.

Conversation	Person	Duration (mins)	Listened w/o Interrupting (Yes or No)	Responded Quickly (Yes or No)	Observations
Ex. Work meeting	Alex	20	No	Yes	Interrupted often; I need to improve my patience

 **Connection:**

Feedback Request: Regularly ask a trusted colleague or friend for specific feedback on your communication after important conversations.

 Growth:

Intentional Practice: Choose a few key phrases to replace common, vague expressions you use, aiming for more clarity and precision.

Public Speaking Practice: Join a local Toastmasters club or volunteer to present at meetings or events. Regular practice in public speaking can enhance clarity, confidence, and your ability to adapt messages to different audiences.

Ally's Something Extra

Ally's communication is uplifting 99.9 percent of the time. I recently dropped her off at the salon for a hair appointment. Our stylist, Brittny, has done our hair since Paige was in middle school, and she is like a big sister to both Paige and Ally.

When I returned to pick Ally up, there were several others in the salon, and Ally had completely taken command of the room in the most beautiful way.

She was asking Brittny about her kids and her husband, Tony. She was telling another customer, Brie, how much she loved her own family. And then without hesitation, Ally told Brie she loved her too.

Brie was nearly teary-eyed when she told me how much Ally had brightened her day. "A ray of sunshine," she said.

Ally's communication is trustworthy, authentic, and credible. If she tells you she likes your blouse, she really does. She's not angling for something. Words like *manipulation* and *flattery* don't even exist in her vocabulary. If she tells you she loves you, she genuinely, deeply does.

Something Extra Podcast

- ► Bill Ellis, episode 154
- ► Bob Tiede, episode 250
- ► Jeremie Kubicek, episode 271
- ► Jason Weems, episode 292

All ?

empowering

empathetic

calmer

adaptable

humble

inspiring

encouraging

approa

PART THREE

PRACTICAL LEADERSHIP

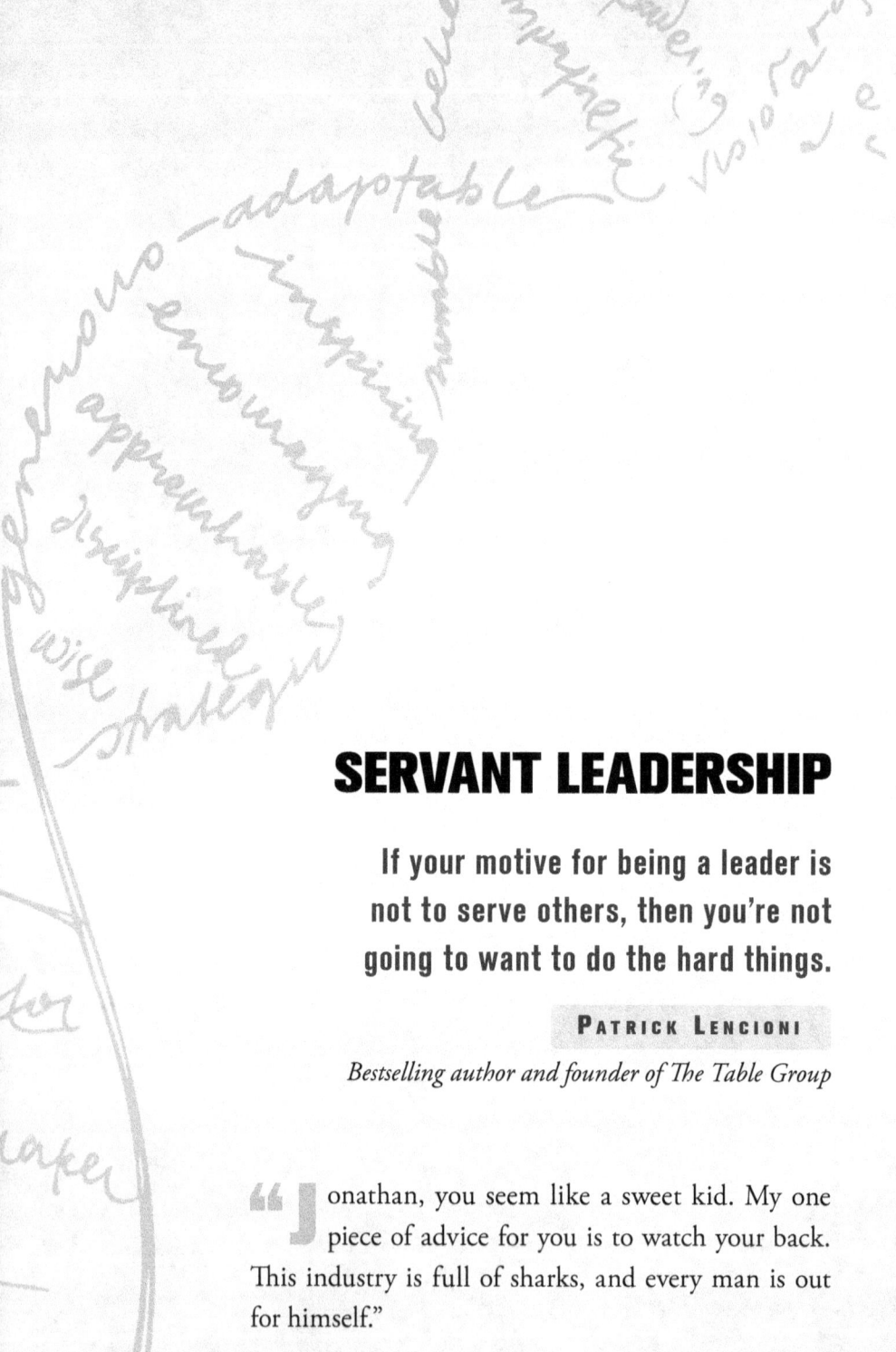

SERVANT LEADERSHIP

If your motive for being a leader is not to serve others, then you're not going to want to do the hard things.

PATRICK LENCIONI

Bestselling author and founder of The Table Group

"Jonathan, you seem like a sweet kid. My one piece of advice for you is to watch your back. This industry is full of sharks, and every man is out for himself."

Jonathan Keyser, his notepad open but untouched, sat across from a seasoned broker. He had been in commercial real estate for less than a year and was still adjusting to the high-stakes nature of the industry. The broker went on. "Nice guys get trampled. You're going to need to look out for number one and play the game if you ever expect to survive in this crazy, vicious industry."

This introduction into the highly competitive world of commercial real estate was a far leap from Jonathan's childhood. He grew up in a home built on serving others. His missionary parents were deeply committed to helping others and living by principles of generosity, faith, and selflessness. Kindness and integrity weren't just ideals; they were a way of life.

As a child, Jonathan absorbed those values, but he also equated them with being poor. His parents taught him what really mattered, but he didn't know how to turn that into dollars. So when commercial real estate was presented as a path toward money and wealth, he took it. And when a company executive urged Jonathan to protect himself and look out for number one, he took the advice to heart. He adapted to his environment, learning to be aggressive, self-serving, and relentlessly focused on winning.

It worked—for a while. Despite Jonathan's growing success, something felt wrong. He had the deals, the numbers, and the respect of his peers in the industry, but deep down, he wasn't happy. He was becoming someone he didn't recognize.

It wasn't until a conference speaker challenged the idea of win at all costs that Jonathan began to believe there was a different way. *What if I don't have to be ruthless to win?* he wondered. The speaker suggested investing in relationships through selfless service, asserting that if you help people rather than always try to get something from them, over time you'll have success. What if Jonathan could actually be successful *and* focus on loving and serving others?

This concept resonated with Jonathan, and after some soul-searching, he decided to reinvent himself. It wasn't an easy road. But as he committed himself to this new philosophy, something surprising happened. Not overnight but with time, clients responded, and his reputation grew. He built a thriving business, not in spite of his selfless approach but because of it. It was counterintuitive in an industry known for its ruthless competition, but success really could come from putting others' needs first.

SERVE WITH HEART

One powerful lesson from Jonathan Keyser is his personal commitment to serving others—every single day. He has made a covenant with himself to daily help at least three people in some meaningful way. While no one can change the entire world all at once, imagine the ripple effect of intentionally impacting just three people each day. Over the course of a lifetime, those small yet consistent acts of service could multiply exponentially, touching thousands if not millions of lives.

This mindset aligns perfectly with the principles of servant leadership that prioritizes lifting others up, fostering meaningful relationships, and creating a culture of generosity. True leadership isn't about personal gain or recognition; it's about making a difference in the lives of those around you. By focusing on serving others in small, intentional ways, we build trust, inspire action, and cultivate a legacy of impact.

If we all adopted this approach, even in a small way, how

much more unified, compassionate, and purpose-driven would our workplaces and communities become?

At Technology Partners, Greg and I both make it a priority to serve our employees, our clients, our community, and beyond. Our employees are not there to serve us; we are there to serve them, and they in turn will serve our clients. We have always believed that if we do right by our employees, they will do right by our clients, and then our success will follow. It is a win-win-win.

MAKE THE COFFEE

Many of my podcast guests speak of servant leadership, and Landon Hobson, CEO of Cosmos Corporation, a pet products company, is one of those.

The company's mission is impressive: *To enrich the lives of our people and pets, support and invest in our employees, and provide for the poor around the globe—all to the glory of God.* They follow up that mission statement with several core values. One of them is to *be willing to make the coffee.* At Cosmos Corporation, they take servant leadership seriously. Employees not only know the company values but see them in action every day. Even as CEO, Landon can often be seen in the company break room making coffee—serving his team.

Cosmos also encourages company and individual mission efforts. Landon says when you go out and serve, you come back into the company more of a servant leader. You take the characteristics and attributes you learn serving others and pour them into your work. Serving others and thinking of others before yourself make a big impact. It really does change the dynamic of a relationship.

Frank Harrison is another CEO who exemplifies servant leadership through his commitment to creating a culture that honors God and serves others. Under his guidance, Coca-Cola Consolidated (the largest Coke bottler in the nation) has as its stated purpose "To honor God in all we do, to serve others, to pursue excellence, and to grow profitably." Coca-Cola Consolidated is a publicly traded company with over 18,000 employees. Frank's mission is to influence 18,000 employees to be servant leaders by emphasizing values and actions that reflect this philosophy. Frank views himself as the "chief steward," accountable for using the company's resources to positively impact their employees, suppliers, and communities.

A few years ago, I had the privilege of speaking to Coca-Cola Consolidated's women's leadership group as well as its customer service and sales teams. During my visit, I was profoundly impressed by the company's commitment to fostering a culture of servant leadership.

A SELFLESS MISSION

Jonathan Keyser continues to focus on selfless service in his commercial real estate business. In 2019, he wrote a *Wall Street Journal* bestselling book, *You Don't Have to Be Ruthless to Win*. Leaving the cutthroat, win-at-all-costs mentality behind, Jonathan is now on a mission to change the commercial real estate industry. He wants to be a light on a hill, shining the message that there is a different way, and if it can be done in his industry, it can be done in any business.

You may not sell commercial real estate or run a company, but the principle of servant leadership applies to whatever arena you find yourself in. Servant leadership is more than a buzzword. Leaders who focus on selfless service can change the world.

Reflection:

1. In a culture that often rewards competition and personal gain, how do you define success in your own life? How does servant leadership challenge or reshape that definition?

2. How do you feel about serving others when there's no immediate reward or recognition?

3. In your current or past jobs, have you worked in an environment that prioritized servant leadership? If so, how did it shape the team dynamics? If not, what would have changed if servant leadership had been embraced?

4. Jonathan Keyser commits to helping three people every day in meaningful ways. What small yet impactful changes could you make in your daily routine?

5. If you were to fully embrace servant leadership, what kind of legacy would you hope to leave behind? How would you want others to describe your leadership and the way you treated people?

 **Action:**

Win-Win Reflection: Identify a situation where you typically compete or focus on personal gain. Write down alternative servant-leader approaches that could create mutual success instead.

PERSONAL GAIN SITUATION	ALTERNATIVE SERVANT LEADER APPROACH
Ex. Being point person on a group project to gain recognition as a leader	*Making note of team members' strengths and asking if someone else wants to take the lead since it's their expertise*

Servant Leadership Journal: Keep a daily or weekly journal where you log intentional acts of service, no matter how small. Reflect on how they impacted you and others. Start here by logging your first full week of acts of service.

Daily Log

Monday:

Tuesday:

Wednesday:

Thursday:

Friday:

Saturday:

Sunday:

 **Connection:**

Three-Person Commitment: Following Jonathan Keyser's example, set a goal to help at least three people each day in a meaningful way. Track who you help and how, and then review patterns over time.

My Three People:

1.

2.

3.

Service Networking: Instead of typical business networking, look for ways to serve others first. In meetings or social settings, focus on asking, "How can I help you?" rather than seeking personal gain.

 Growth:

Servant Leadership Case Study: Research a leader known for servant leadership (e.g., Mother Teresa, Nelson Mandela, a business leader like Howard Schultz). Identify three key takeaways and apply them to your leadership approach.

Morning Intentions and Evening Reflections: Each morning, set an intention for how you will practice servant leadership that day. In the evening, reflect on whether you followed through and what you learned.

 Something Extra Podcast

- ▶ Jonathan Keyser, episode 160
- ▶ Landon Hobson, episode 194
- ▶ Patrick Lencioni, episode 300

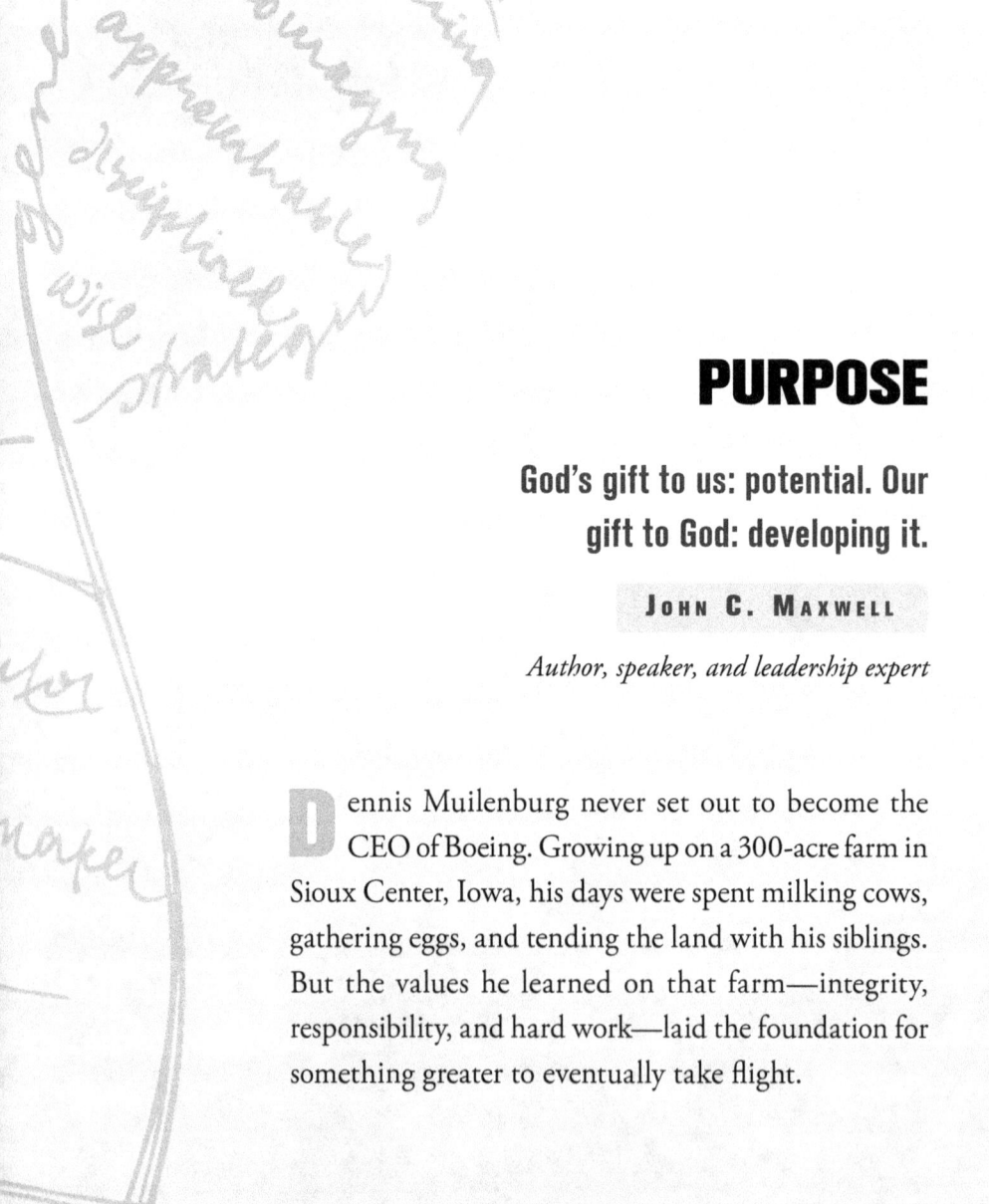

PURPOSE

God's gift to us: potential. Our gift to God: developing it.

JOHN C. MAXWELL

Author, speaker, and leadership expert

Dennis Muilenburg never set out to become the CEO of Boeing. Growing up on a 300-acre farm in Sioux Center, Iowa, his days were spent milking cows, gathering eggs, and tending the land with his siblings. But the values he learned on that farm—integrity, responsibility, and hard work—laid the foundation for something greater to eventually take flight.

Dennis followed his childhood fascination with the sky to Iowa State University where he studied aerospace engineering. The vast expanse above his family's fields had sparked a dream that eventually led him to Boeing where he began as an aerodynamicist, designing planes with the quiet joy that comes when talent meets purpose.

Purpose isn't static, and over time, Dennis discovered that even more than designing aircraft, his deeper calling was to build people. He stepped into leadership not because he chased a title but because he was drawn to the multiplying effect of empowering teams.

Dennis once said that you have to make the best use of the talents God has given you in the purpose He's given you. That belief not only guided Dennis's leadership at one of the world's largest aerospace companies but also fueled his passion for mentoring others.

Purpose is the quiet pull that guides our choices, the standard that shapes our leadership, and the reason we keep showing up with integrity, especially when no one is watching.

Dennis's journey reminds us that true purpose begins in the small, often unseen places, whether that's on the family farm, in an engineering lab, or in a leadership position. Our sense of purpose grows when we steward our gifts with humility and excellence.

In a world that often measures success by status, purpose invites us to measure it by service. Who are we lifting? What legacy are we leaving? Are we building something that will outlast us?

PURPOSEFUL USE OF TIME

My own purpose is deeply tied to trying to be the most effective business leader I can be and, more importantly, glorifying God. Colossians 3:23 says, "Whatever you do, work at it with all your heart, as working for the Lord, not for human masters."

This verse encourages us to approach everything we do—whether work, service, or any given responsibility—with dedication and excellence as though we are doing it for God Himself rather than for human approval or reward. It speaks to the idea of serving God wholeheartedly in all areas of life, with a focus on pleasing and honoring Him above all.

Jordan Raynor is an entrepreneur, author, and speaker who embodies the importance of living with purpose, particularly concerning work and faith.

His book *Redeeming Your Time: 7 Biblical Principles for Being Purposeful, Present & Wildly Productive* offers a faith-based approach to time management, productivity, and purpose. When I hosted Jordan on my podcast, we spoke in depth about his book and especially the intersection of *workspace productivity* and *grace-based productivity*.

I hadn't heard of those phrases—*workspace productivity* and *grace-based productivity*—prior to talking with Jordan. Workspace productivity is what the world can offer us in the form of time management books. In fact, there are currently 60,000 of them on Amazon to choose from. These books promise that during an overwhelming season of stress, we need to simply follow their system, and just like that, everything will work out. And you will have peace.

The truth is we must find peace in something that is more secure. That is where grace-based productivity comes into play. Grace-based productivity is protected by a greater purpose.

Jordan says, "I don't do time management exercises in a wild goose chase to get peace. I do it in response to the foundational secure peace that I've already been given and found in a secure place—the books of Matthew, Mark, Luke, and John. The Bible doesn't show these men with a calendar or a to-do list, but they do show Jesus seeking solitude so He could think clearly and be creative."

Throughout His earthly ministry, Jesus often found Himself surrounded by crowds as He was teaching, healing, and performing miracles. His life was filled with constant demands on His time and energy. Yet in the midst of this, Jesus intentionally sought moments of solitude to commune with His Heavenly Father. He modeled the importance of soul-care by withdrawing from the noise and busyness to find rest in God's presence.

Jordan told me he has dedicated his life to helping people respond to truth and redeem their time. "If we believe our work matters deeply, then we should care about stewarding our time as wisely as humanly possible," he said. Just the day before our conversation, I had written this in my journal: *God, help me to steward the time you have given me.* I know better than to believe that the timing of this journal entry was a coincidence.

As a way of redeeming the time, Jordan says that when we align our professional goals with a higher purpose, we not only find deeper fulfillment but also make a more meaningful impact on the world. A strong sense of purpose helps guide career decisions and fosters a mindset of stewardship—seeing our talents, time, and resources as gifts to be used wisely. Jordan encourages people to seek clarity in their mission by reflecting on their unique strengths and passions and thinking about how they can best serve others. Being intentional about our work turns it into an act of worship and a way to make a lasting difference, both spiritually and practically.

I fully believe that every human being is created for a purpose. And that purpose is not to serve ourselves but to make the world a better place by using the unique gifts we've been given to uplift, inspire, and contribute to something greater than ourselves.

When we embrace our gifts and intentionally share them, we create a ripple effect that extends far beyond what we can see. A kind word, a selfless act, a moment of encouragement—these things may seem small, but their impact is immeasurable. We may never fully realize this side of heaven how many lives we've touched simply by walking in our purpose.

That belief is what inspired me to create the *Something Extra* podcast. I wanted to highlight leaders who are using their gifts to influence their industries, communities, and the world in meaningful ways. By sharing their stories, my hope is to inspire others because when we all step into our purpose, the world becomes a brighter, more connected, and more compassionate place.

PURPOSEFUL LEADERSHIP

John C. Maxwell is a well-known Christian leadership expert, speaker, and author who emphasizes the importance of purpose-driven leadership. In his many books, such as *The 21 Irrefutable Laws of Leadership* and *Intentional Living: Choosing a Life That Matters*, John talks about living with purpose and making intentional choices in leadership and life.

"Success is knowing your purpose in life, growing to reach your maximum potential, and sowing seeds that benefit others," John says.

Leadership is not just about personal achievement but about adding value to others. To lead effectively, John emphasizes the importance of having a clear sense of purpose. He encourages leaders to live intentionally, understanding that intentionality is key to realizing your God-given potential and creating a meaningful, positive impact on the lives of others.

Studies show that purpose is not just a personal value but a business driver, improving employee satisfaction, retention, innovation, and long-term organizational success. Workplace engagement, individual well-being, business performance, talent attraction, and retention are just a few of the indicators of a work environment that fosters a culture of purpose.

In a study reported in 2020, McKinsey & Company found that leaders who articulate a strong personal and organizational purpose foster higher employee morale, stronger performance, and greater loyalty. In the survey, 82 percent of executives who strongly align with their company's purpose reported a high level of leadership satisfaction and effectiveness.[1]

A study published in *Psychological Science* revealed that individuals with a strong sense of purpose tend to live longer, healthier lives. Participants with a sense of purpose were found to have a 15 percent lower risk of death compared to those who lacked a clear purpose.[2]

Living purposefully means making decisions that reflect your core values and long-term goals. As both a mother and a business leader, I believe my God-given purpose serves as the foundation for all I do. Whether at home or in the workplace, my faith shapes my why, guiding every choice I make.

In business, my goal is to create value, lead with integrity, and positively influence others in a way that honors God's calling. At home, my focus is on raising my children to grow in character, honor God, and serve others. In both areas, faith and purpose keep me grounded, intentional, and committed to a higher calling.

Purpose is the anchor that steers us through personal and professional paths, fostering self-governance and aligning our actions with deeper values. Whether leading in business or at home, a purpose rooted in faith provides clarity and direction. Aligning our work with faith enables us to lead intentionally and make a lasting impact. In all areas of life, purpose drives us to lead with integrity, inspire others, and create meaningful change.

Reflection:

....

1. Looking back, what are some defining moments that changed your perspective on what truly matters?

2. If you had unlimited resources and no fear of failure, how would you spend your time to create meaning in the world?

3. What problems or injustices in the world stir something deep within you and make you want to take action?

4. Where do you feel most aligned with your purpose, and where do you feel misaligned? How does your current work or daily life reflect your deeper sense of purpose?

5. If you had to summarize your purpose in one sentence, what would it be?

Action:

Past Patterns Review: Make a timeline of five key life events, challenges, and moments of fulfillment. Look for recurring themes that point to your deeper purpose.

$$\longrightarrow$$

LIFE TIMELINE

Purpose : List your daily activities and commitments. Identify which ones align with your purpose.

DAILY ACTIVITIES	Check If Aligns with Purpose
Ex. 2-mile run in the morning	

Connection:

....

Service Reflection: Volunteer for a cause that resonates with you. Afterward, journal about how it reinforced or reshaped your understanding of purpose.

Networking with Purpose: Connect with people who inspire you and live with purpose. Ask about their journey and lessons they've learned. Make a list of five people you'd like to connect with.

1. _____

2. _____

3. _____

4. _____

5. _____

 ## Growth:
....

Mindset Shift Challenge: For one week, intentionally reframe daily tasks as opportunities to live out your purpose, even in small ways.

Skill-Building for Purpose: Identify a skill or knowledge area that will help you fulfill your purpose more effectively and commit to learning it.

 ### Something Extra Podcast
....

► Dennis Muilenburg, episode 93
► Jordan Raynor, episode 179

VISION

The only thing worse than being blind is having sight but no vision.

HELEN KELLER

Author and disability rights advocate

D ebbie Morris was twenty-five years old when her body gave out on her. Lying in a hospital bed, too weak to sit up, she watched as doctors hovered over her, speaking in hushed tones. Confused and terrified, she tried to piece together how she had ended up there.

Just days before, she had been grinding through another high-stress, high-stakes day in the finance industry—long hours, little sleep, and even less concern for her well-being. But now, her body had forced her to stop. Doctors diagnosed her with a severe autoimmune disorder, warning her that unless she made drastic changes, her future would be filled with hospital stays, medications, and limitations.

For the first time, Debbie was forced to ask herself, *Is this the life I really want?*

Debbie had once been the picture of health and discipline. Her father—an athlete and fitness enthusiast—had instilled in her a love for strength, movement, and proper nutrition. As a child, she lifted weights alongside him, played sports, and even ordered the healthiest meals at restaurants just to follow his example.

But somewhere along the way, Debbie lost sight of that vision. The pursuit of career success overshadowed her foundational values. Her life had become a relentless chase for achievement, status, and financial security, but at what cost?

Lying in that hospital bed, it became clear that something had to change. "What you learn really fast when your health fails you is that it doesn't matter how much money or power you have," Debbie said.

Her vision for her life had been consumed by external success. Now she needed a vision that prioritized who she wanted to be—not just what she wanted to achieve.

FINDING A NEW PATH

Debbie's journey to healing wasn't quick or easy. It took two years, twenty-three doctors, and countless moments of frustration before she began to feel whole again. But in that season of searching, she found something far more valuable—her faith and a renewed purpose.

At her lowest point, she made a promise. "God, if you are real, I will live the rest of my life for You. If You show me how to get better and You show me the path to healing, I'll dedicate everything I do to You."

From that moment forward, she pursued a new vision—one rooted in faith, health, and serving others. She read the Bible cover to cover, deepened her relationship with God, and was baptized. Her healing became more than just physical. It was spiritual, mental, and emotional. And with each step forward, a new vision for her life took shape.

Today, Debbie is a thriving entrepreneur, speaker, and fitness professional. She founded Integrity Training Systems where a chance encounter led her to John—now her husband and business partner. Together, they empower others to reclaim their health through functional fitness and nutrition. John leads the fitness trainers and coaches, and Debbie focuses on nutritional training, ensuring a well-rounded approach to wellness.

Their passion extends beyond the gym. They cohost *Faith, Fuel, & Fitness – The Integrity Way*, a radio show dedicated to guiding others toward holistic well-being. United by a shared vision, Debbie and John are committed to helping people become the best versions of themselves—physically, mentally, and spiritually.

But what truly sets Debbie apart isn't just her expertise; it's her unwavering vision.

She knows that true transformation begins with a clear, guiding vision. It's not just about setting goals; it's about knowing why you're pursuing them in the first place.

When you have a clear vision, it becomes your North Star, guiding your decisions, actions, and priorities. It gives you purpose, direction, and the resilience to persevere through challenges.

As Proverbs 29:18 (KJV) reminds us, "Where there is no vision, the people perish." Without a vision bigger than yourself, it's too easy to lose focus, drift aimlessly, and never fully understand your purpose. But when your vision is strong and deeply rooted, it fuels your passion, keeps you grounded in your values, and propels you forward—even in the face of adversity and setbacks. It gives meaning to the journey, helping you stay steadfast and intentional in every step you take.

I also think about the Cheshire Cat in *Alice's Adventures in Wonderland* who said, "If you don't know where you're going, any road will take you there." Having a clear vision is crucial. It ensures that we are not merely reacting to life but actively shaping our path with intention and purpose. Without vision, we risk wandering through life without direction, settling for less than we are capable of and missing out on the impact we were meant to make.

THE POWER OF VISION: A STORY OF BREAKTHROUGH

When Greg and I dated in high school, he didn't know exactly how the dots would connect, but he had a vision. "Lisa, if we build a successful company, we can do a lot of good in the world."

For over thirty years, we've stayed true to that vision, using our success to uplift our team, clients, and communities. Together, we've helped fund hundreds of nonprofits and community initiatives, bringing our team immense joy and purpose.

But vision isn't reserved for business leaders or those with abundant resources. Sometimes it's found in the most unlikely places, like a mother in Kenya living on just $2 a day. For Naomi, survival was a daily battle, and the weight of generational poverty seemed inescapable. But she refused to accept that her children's future had to look like her past.

Naomi had a vision bigger than herself.

Determined to change the trajectory of her children's lives, she approached her church—not for a handout, but for a loan. She wanted to start a small business that could sustain her family. That one decision changed everything.

Not only did she successfully launch her business, but it thrived, allowing her to send her children to school. One of them, Lillian, went on to graduate from the University of Nairobi with a degree in economic development. Inspired by her mother's resilience, Lillian Covington has devoted her life to giving others a hand—just like her mother Naomi did—and helping people change the trajectory of their lives, not just for themselves but for generations to come.

Lillian happens to be a dear friend who now works for Opportunity International (OI), a global nonprofit that focuses on empowering people who are living in poverty. Greg and I have been privileged to serve on OI's Board of Governors for many years, and Atul Tandon, CEO of OI, was one of my earliest podcast guests.

At its heart, OI's mission is to give individuals—especially women—the tools they need to build sustainable livelihoods, send their children to school, and transform their communities. Founded in 1971 by Al Whittaker, former president of Bristol-Myers; and David Bussau, an Australian entrepreneur, OI focuses on microfinance. They offer small loans, savings accounts, insurance, and training to people who don't have access to traditional banking systems. They also invest heavily in education and agricultural initiatives.

They work in over thirty countries with a strong presence in Africa, Latin America, Asia, and Eastern Europe. Thanks to the resources OI provides, millions of people have been able to start or expand businesses, create jobs, and break cycles of poverty, all while building dignity, responsibility, and self-sufficiency.

Years ago, Lillian's mother, Naomi, had every reason to give up. But her vision was more powerful than her circumstances. Indirectly, that vision has had a ripple effect across multiple generations and around the world.

HOW TO CLARIFY YOUR OWN VISION

A clear vision is the foundation for a meaningful life. It's what guides your decisions, fuels your perseverance, and gives your work a sense of purpose.

If you feel lost—like Debbie did in her hospital bed—consider these questions:

- ▷ Who do I want to become?
- ▷ What values do I refuse to compromise?
- ▷ If I removed all external pressures (money, status, expectations), what would I truly pursue?
- ▷ What impact do I want to make?

Vision isn't just about what you achieve; it's about who you are becoming along the way.

Debbie's vision shifted from financial success to faith-driven wellness. Naomi's vision shifted from daily survival to breaking generational poverty. Our vision at Technology Partners is making a global impact by harnessing technology for the greater good.

My personal vision closely aligns with this. I am committed to leaving every person in my sphere of influence better than I found them through intentional support, encouraging words, and purposeful actions. I strive to uplift, inspire, and equip others to reach their full potential, whether through mentorship, encouragement, or simply leading by example. By living with purpose, authenticity, and a servant-leader mindset, I hope to help create a world where people feel valued, empowered, seen, and loved.

What vision will shape your future?

Reflection:

....

1. Have you ever been part of a team, company, or community where a shared vision made a significant difference? How did that collective vision affect morale, productivity, and success?

2. What makes you feel fulfilled? (Examples could be material success, achieving a personal or professional goal, or impacting another person's life for the better.)

3. What is your current vision for your life? Write it out in one or two sentences. Be focused and concise.

4. Does your vision align with your values, passions, and faith? If so, how?

5. How does your vision impact the people around you—family, friends, colleagues, and your community? Are you creating a positive influence and inspiring others, or are you too focused on personal ambitions at the expense of meaningful connections?

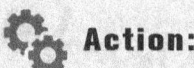 **Action:**

Strengths and Passions Inventory: Fill out the chart below. In the first column, identify your natural talents. In the second column, list things you love to do and are passionate about. Look for overlap and consider how these can guide your vision.

MY STRENGTHS AND TALENTS	MY PASSIONS	MY VISION
Ex. I'm a talented piano player.	I enjoy live music and performing.	I could hold a concert to benefit the local women's shelter.

Your Top Five Moments: List the top five moments in your life when you felt the most fulfilled, inspired, or accomplished. Analyze what made those moments meaningful and what they reveal about your purpose.

MY TOP FIVE MOMENTS

1.

2.

3.

4.

5.

No Distractions: Spend a day alone without distractions—no phone, no media, just a notebook and your thoughts. Journal about what truly matters to you, what legacy you want to leave, and what would make your life feel meaningful.

Connection:

Coffee Shop Chat: Invite three people who know you well (friends, family, mentors) to individual coffee chats. Ask them what they see as your greatest strengths and what they believe you're meant to do. Compare their insights with your own reflections.

Surround Yourself with the Right Mentors: Seek accountability by finding a mentor, coach, or mastermind group that can help refine and strengthen your vision. Set regular check-ins to discuss progress and challenges.

Be a Passionate Volunteer: Find a way to contribute to your community in a way that aligns with your vision, whether through volunteering, mentoring, or starting a small initiative that reflects your purpose.

Growth:

Define Your Perfect Day: Write a "perfect day" exercise where you describe in detail what your ideal day looks like five years from now. Include where you are, what you're doing, who you're with, and how you feel. Look for patterns that reveal your deepest desires.

Thirty-Day Vision Challenge: Take one small action every day that aligns with your vision. Reflect on how these actions shape your mindset and progress toward your goals. Track your action each day to hold yourself accountable for your growth.

Something Extra Podcast

- ► Atul Tandon, episode 2
- ► Debbie Morris, episode 228

INFLUENCE

The key to successful leadership today is influence, not authority.

KEN BLANCHARD

Bestselling author and leadership expert

A few years ago, Jon Gordon, a multiple-time bestselling author and renowned speaker, delivered the keynote address at the National Leadership Academy, a nonprofit organization founded by my friend Tommy Spaulding. The words Jon delivered from the podium carried the kind of weight that stops you in your tracks, the kind that lingers long after the applause fades and the room empties.

"I heard about a recent study showing that the average person will influence eighty thousand people in their lifetime, positively or negatively," Jon said.

Eighty thousand.

If you break it down, that's about three people a day—three opportunities every single day to uplift, encourage, and show genuine care for another human being.

This revelation consumed Tommy. He started picturing the great stadiums of the world packed to capacity with 80,000 faces. Then he imagined *what if, at the end of your life, one of those stadiums was filled with the people you influenced?* They could be the colleagues you worked alongside, the friends you shared life with, the stranger in line at the grocery store, the seatmate on a long flight, the delivery driver, or the neighbor you waved to but never really knew. And of course, they could be your family.

How would their lives have been shaped—for better or worse—simply because they crossed paths with you?

Tommy couldn't shake the question. It moved him so profoundly that it became the heartbeat of his bestselling book *The Gift of Influence.*

"The 80,000 people in your stadium won't remember your title," Tommy says. "They won't remember the products you sold or the services you provided. But they will remember the words you spoke and the actions you took that changed their lives."

In his book, Tommy emphasizes several key points, but three main themes stand out.

➤ The power of asking "What's your story?"

⯈ The secret to turning transactions into true interactions.

⯈ Showing up meaningfully for people in need instead of saying, "Let me know how I can help."

In the end, influence isn't about status; it's about significance. It's about the unseen ripple effect of a kind word spoken in a moment of doubt, a simple act of generosity that shifts someone's perspective, or the decision to show up when it would have been easier to walk away. It's about choosing to be a source of light in a world that so often leans toward darkness.

I believe that influence is the seed, and impact is the fruit. Influence shapes thoughts, behaviors, and decisions, while impact is the tangible change that grows from that influence.

From the very beginning of Technology Partners, Greg and I have been guided by our faith—not just in what we do but in how and why we do it. Scripture shaped our foundational principles. It led us to lead with integrity, serve with humility, and pursue excellence in everything we do. It became the framework for our innovative business model—one that has stood the test of time for more than thirty years.

It also helped us define the core values that continue to serve as the bedrock of Technology Partners today.

⯈ Do things right
⯈ Exceed expectations
⯈ Learn and share
⯈ Innovate and transform
⯈ Grow as individuals
⯈ Help others
⯈ Trust and be transparent

Building a business has never been just about personal success. From the beginning, it has been about creating wins—for our employees, our clients, and the communities we serve. Our goal has always been to build a company that operates the right way because it's a calling, not just a career.

That belief has influenced every decision, from how we treat our team and clients to the standards we uphold in our work.

Jesus came to serve, not to be served, and we believe true leadership is rooted in service. Our mission has always been to lead with integrity, humility, and a commitment to making a meaningful impact. As we continue this journey, we remain dedicated to building a business that reflects these values—one that lifts others, creates opportunities, and leaves a lasting legacy of excellence and service.

THE INFLUENCE OF A HELPER'S HEART

Names carry weight. Alexandra Alyse, or "Ally" as we call her, has a name rich with meaning—helper of mankind, dedicated to God. And if ever a name fits a soul, it's hers.

From the time she was little, Ally has had an innate pull toward helping, not because she was told to but because it was simply who she was. Some people try to influence others through their words, their titles, or their status. But Ally? She influences through quiet, unwavering action.

When we founded our company three decades ago, we quickly learned the value of delegation. We made it a priority to entrust necessary but nonstrategic tasks to others, a decision that became an unexpected blessing. It allowed us to focus more on family when we weren't working, while also creating opportunities for college students who joined us part-time as family assistants. They weren't just helpers; they became like daughters to us and big sisters to Ally.

And in that way, influence began to take root—not in grand gestures but in the way these young women became part of the fabric of our family. They shaped Ally's view of service, leadership, and what it means to step in and make a difference.

Then COVID hit.

With both Ally and our middle daughter, Paige, being immunocompromised, we had to make the difficult decision to pause having family assistants in our home. The absence was deeply felt. The familiar rhythm of shared responsibilities suddenly shifted, leaving a void where laughter and extra helping hands used to be.

And that's when Ally, true to her name, stepped in.

Without hesitation, she became the family assistant—not just in title, but in heart. She moved through the days with quiet diligence, scanning the house for ways to lighten our load. Laundry? Done. Dogs? Fed. Trash? Emptied. When Paige was unwell, Ally instinctively became her nurse. She didn't wait to be asked. She simply saw, stepped up, and did.

She may not have realized it at the time, but her influence was unmistakable.

Real influence isn't about control; it's about presence. It's about seeing a need and filling it. It's about showing up, not for recognition but because it matters.

And that is exactly what Ally did. It wasn't just about completing tasks; it was about the pride she took in them. It was the way she found joy in serving, in making life a little easier for those around her.

And now, when she meets someone new, her introduction is

never just "I'm Ally." She stands a little taller, smiles a little wider, and says with unmistakable pride, "I'm the family assistant."

It's a title she wears like a badge of honor, a role she's made entirely her own.

Our daughter, Ally, exudes this trait.

THE RIPPLE EFFECT OF INFLUENCE

The most remarkable thing about influence is that it doesn't stop with you. Just like a single pebble can create endless ripples in a pond, a single act of selfless influence can reach farther than you'll ever know.

Imagine a world where influence wasn't about control but about contribution where people focused less on their own success and more on helping others succeed. Imagine a world where every interaction—big or small—was approached with this question: *How can I add value to this person's life today?*

What kind of impact would that have on your relationships, your business, your leadership, and your legacy?

In the end, influence isn't measured by the number of followers, the size of a paycheck, or the accolades earned. Influence is measured by the lives we touch, the people we uplift, and the significance we leave behind.

It all starts with putting others first.

And in that, influence continues, reminding all of us that sometimes the most profound impact doesn't come from a stage or a position of power. It comes from the quiet, steady hands of those who choose to serve.

So this question remains: What kind of influence will you leave behind? If you could stand in that stadium at the end of your life, looking into the faces of those you impacted, would you be proud of the legacy you created?

Every day—three times a day—you have the chance to write that story.

And maybe, just maybe, someone else will sit in an audience years from now, hear about the power of influence, and think of you.

Reflection:

....

1. Who has been one of the most influential people in your life? What
    lasting impact did they have on you?

2. Who in your life is quietly watching how you live? What are
    they learning?

3. In your current season of life, who are the "three faces a day" within your reach? (Think about family, coworkers, friends.) How intentional are you about uplifting or positively impacting them?

4. Where in your life do you hold influence but haven't fully stepped into it yet?

5. When you imagine your own "stadium of eighty thousand," what do you hope people will remember you for? How do you hope you've influenced them?

⚙ Action:

Influence : Scroll through recent text conversations and emails. Highlight messages where you encouraged, supported, advised, or impacted someone. Then count how many of those were intentional versus unintentional.

Social Media Reflection: Review your last ten posts or comments online. What kind of influence are you projecting? Are you adding value, creating connection, or unintentionally affecting others in ways you didn't intend?

Ripple Chart: Pick one recent action, word, or decision. Create a ripple diagram to trace its direct and indirect impact—who it affected, how it spread, and what outcomes followed.

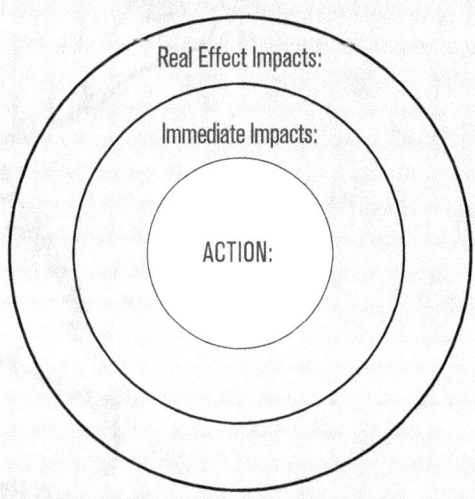

Real Effect Impacts:

Immediate Impacts:

ACTION:

 **Connection:** ....

Three Areas of Influence: Consider the chart below labeled Personal, Professional, and Community. Fill in the names of people you influence in each, and then reflect. Where are you most engaged? Least engaged? What connections surprise you?

PERSONAL	PROFESSIONAL	COMMUNITY
Ex. My children	*Ex. My boss*	*Ex. My neighbor*

Growth:

Stadium Snapshot: Below is your stadium with room for eighty thousand people. Write the names of twenty people you've definitely influenced and leave the rest blank, representing the unknown connections still to come. Reflect on how many faces you'll never realize you touched.

MY STADIUM OF INFLUENCE

 Something Extra Podcast

► Ken Blanchard, episode 200
► Tommy Spaulding, episode 306

LEADERSHIP CULTURE

Culture eats strategy for breakfast.

PETER DRUCKER

Management expert

B ack in the 1970s in Atlanta, Georgia, Mark Miller wasn't just a struggling team member in the kitchen at Chick-fil-A. He was a self-professed *awful* team member. He was so bad, in fact, that when he realized he was on the verge of being fired, he made a split-second decision to quit first, sparing himself the embarrassment of being let go.

But this hasty, preemptive departure only left him in a tailspin of finding the next job. And he did, only to be laid off just six months later. Desperate for work, he thought back to his short-lived stint at Chick-fil-A. He hadn't been a great employee, but he liked the people and the *culture.* There was something about it that had Mark's wheels turning.

This idea came to him: If he couldn't succeed in the kitchen, maybe there was a place for him at corporate headquarters.

The idea became a pivotal next step in Mark's career. He decided to go for it.

Nervous but determined, he approached the front doors, his palms slick with sweat. He approached the receptionist's desk, his heart pounding. She greeted him warmly and asked for his name and the purpose of his visit. As he took a seat in the lobby, he had no idea that fate was about to intervene in the most unexpected way.

Minutes later, the internal lobby door opened, not to reveal a hiring manager or a warehouse supervisor but the founder of Chick-fil-A himself, Truett Cathy.

The interview went well, and Mark was thrilled to learn he was being considered for a role in the warehouse as Chick-fil-A's sixteenth corporate employee.

By some mix of divine grace and Truett's willingness to take a chance on an employee who didn't exactly work out the first time, Mark got the job, and that improbable moment shaped the next forty-plus years of his career with Chick-fil-A.

Over the next four decades, Mark's journey at Chick-fil-A was anything but ordinary. What began as a humble role in the warehouse quickly evolved into a career defined by growth, innovation, and leadership. As a young professional, he didn't just climb the corporate ladder; he built new rungs along the way.

He launched the corporate communications department, shaped

the company's approach to consumer satisfaction, and became the vice president of High Performance Leadership. Mark was the driving force behind cultivating a culture of exceptional leadership.

As the organization grew, Mark took on various roles, each contributing to the strong infrastructure that supports Chick-fil-A today. From the back room to the board room, Mark's career is a testament to the power of vision, adaptability, and a relentless commitment to fostering an excellent culture.

"I don't think this had much to do with my talent or skills. I think it was more 'let the kid do it' because I would do anything," he explained.

Mark's deep passion for leadership development is a key reason that Chick-fil-A has become renowned for cultivating an exceptional leadership culture.

DESIGNING CULTURE

I had the privilege of sitting down with Mark on the *Something Extra* podcast for an insightful conversation about the leadership culture within Chick-fil-A.

"About twenty-five years ago, we began to see cracks in our system," he said. "The way we had developed leaders prior to that time was something I see in a lot of organizations, and it's a process of immersion and osmosis."

As a result of this trial-by-fire approach, the organization lacked *exceptional* leadership. The executive team, recognizing this challenge, entrusted Mark with the mission of accelerating leadership development. What started as a side passion, driven by his belief in the transformative power of strong leadership, soon became his life's work, shaping the very culture of the organization.

That journey ultimately led him to share his insights with the world. As of today, Mark has written ten books. Over one million copies have been printed in twenty-five languages.

For many leaders, culture is like the air they breathe—essential but often taken for granted. They know it matters. In fact, 72 percent of leaders say culture is the most powerful tool they have to drive performance. And yet when asked to rank their priorities, building and maintaining culture landed at number twelve. That disconnect is exactly what Mark set out to address in one of his bestselling books, *Culture Rules*.

Through extensive research across ten countries and conversations with over six thousand leaders and frontline employees, Mark identified a simple but powerful truth: Great cultures don't happen by accident; they happen by design.

And leaders are the architects.

CORE VALUES AND HIGH-PERFORMANCE LEADERSHIP

At Technology Partners, we view culture as a journey rather than a destination. We recognize that building a healthy culture requires constant attention, honest reflection, and commitment from everyone. It's a path we walk together every day.

Our core values serve as our foundation and guideposts. These values aren't just words on a wall or statements in a handbook. They're the principles that guide our decisions, shape our interactions, and define who we are as an organization. They become especially important during times of change and growth.

The culture we nurture internally directly shapes the experience we provide to our clients, consultants, and community. That's why we invest in it daily through meaningful conversations, thoughtful decisions, and mutual accountability. We understand that what happens within our walls reverberates beyond them.

We believe that a strong culture is created collectively. Each team member contributes to the environment we share, whether through small daily interactions or significant leadership decisions. When aligned with our values, these contributions strengthen our foundation. When misaligned, they prompt necessary reflection and course correction.

At Technology Partners, we recognize that the strength of our culture isn't measured by perfection but by how we respond when we fall short of our ideals. It's in these moments that we learn, adapt, and recommit to the values that define us. Every challenge becomes an opportunity for growth when approached with humility and openness.

Culture is dynamic. It evolves as we evolve, requiring consistent attention and care. Sometimes that means celebrating our successes; other times, it means having difficult conversations about where we need to improve. Both are essential parts of the journey.

While we strive to embody our values in every interaction, we acknowledge that this is an ongoing process with both achievements and setbacks along the way. We may not always get it right, but we will always strive to learn from our experiences and move forward with renewed purpose and clarity.

Culture, for better or worse, becomes a legacy that shapes a company for generations. It influences not just employees but their families and the communities they touch. So ask yourself this: *Is the leadership culture I promote one that will stand the test of time in a positive and meaningful way? Am I truly proud of the environment I'm creating for our greatest asset—our people?*

Because in the end, culture isn't just a strategy. It's a choice, a responsibility, and a legacy we build every single day.

Reflection:

••

1. How would you describe "leadership culture" in your own words?
    What does it actually look or feel like when it's done well?

2. Think back. Have you ever worked somewhere with a really bad
    leadership culture? How did it affect you?

3. What behaviors or habits have you seen that quietly set the tone for culture, even if no one talks about them?

4. What's the tone or vibe of leadership in your current workplace? How does it show up day to day?

5. What do you think builds trust the fastest in a team? And what erodes it just as quickly?

6. What role do you play in contributing to a positive leadership culture?

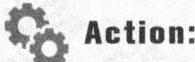 **Action:**

Leadership Culture Snapshot: Create a quick culture chart of your current team or organization. Use three columns: *What We Say*, *What We Do*, and *What People Feel*. Then reflect on how aligned they are.

WHAT WE SAY	WHAT WE DO	WHAT PEOPLE FEEL
Ex. We value transparency.	*Leadership shares big updates but avoids tough conversations.*	*People feel like they're not getting the full story.*

Leadership Culture Self-Rank: Rate yourself in each area from **1 to 5**.

1 = Rarely
2 = Sometimes
3 = Neutral/Inconsistent
4 = Often
5 = Consistently

Then reflect. Where are you showing up strong? Where could you grow?

Modeling Values: *I consistently act in ways that reflect our stated values, even when it's inconvenient or no one's watching.*

Rank

Supporting Others' Growth: *I actively create space for others to learn, grow, and lead, whether through coaching, feedback, or encouragement.*

Rank

Holding to Standards: *I help maintain high standards for performance, behavior, and alignment with culture, even when it's uncomfortable.*

Rank

Creating Safe Spaces: *People feel safe being honest, asking questions, and making mistakes around me without fear of judgment or backlash.*

Rank

Being Culture-Conscious: *I actively think about how my actions and words shape the leadership culture, not just outcomes or tasks.*

Rank

 **Connection:**

Personal Influence Chart: Visualize where you have influence in your world and reflect on how your actions, presence, and leadership choices shape the culture in those spaces. Around the "Me" circle below, label the other four circles for any groups, relationships, or environments you're part of. They can include the following:

- ▶ Your direct team at work
- ▶ Cross-functional colleagues
- ▶ Family or close friends
- ▶ Clients or customers
- ▶ Volunteers
- ▶ Leadership you report to

In each circle, describe how you think your behavior, tone, decisions, or attitude *contribute* to that culture. Are you reinforcing trust, transparency, and accountability, or are you maybe unintentionally undermining it?

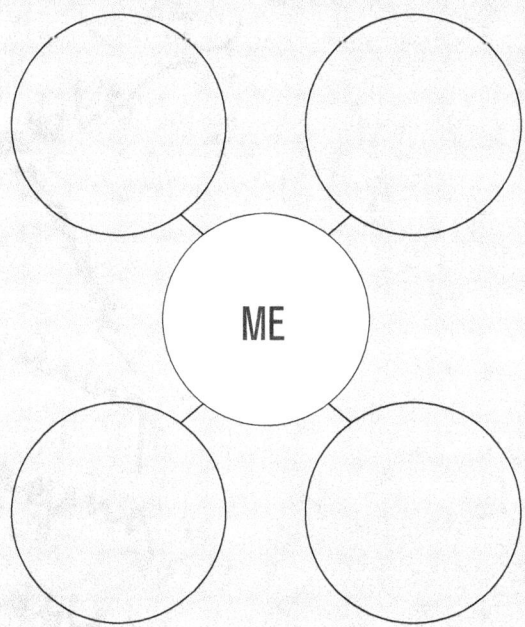

 Growth:

....

Future Culture Vision: Imagine it's two years from now and you've helped shape an exceptional leadership culture. What does it look like? What changed? What did *you* do to help get there?

 Something Extra Podcast

....

► Mark Miller, episode 226

empowering voice

empathetic

values

adaptable

humble

inspiring

encouraging

approach

PART FOUR

KEEP GOING FOR THE LONG HAUL

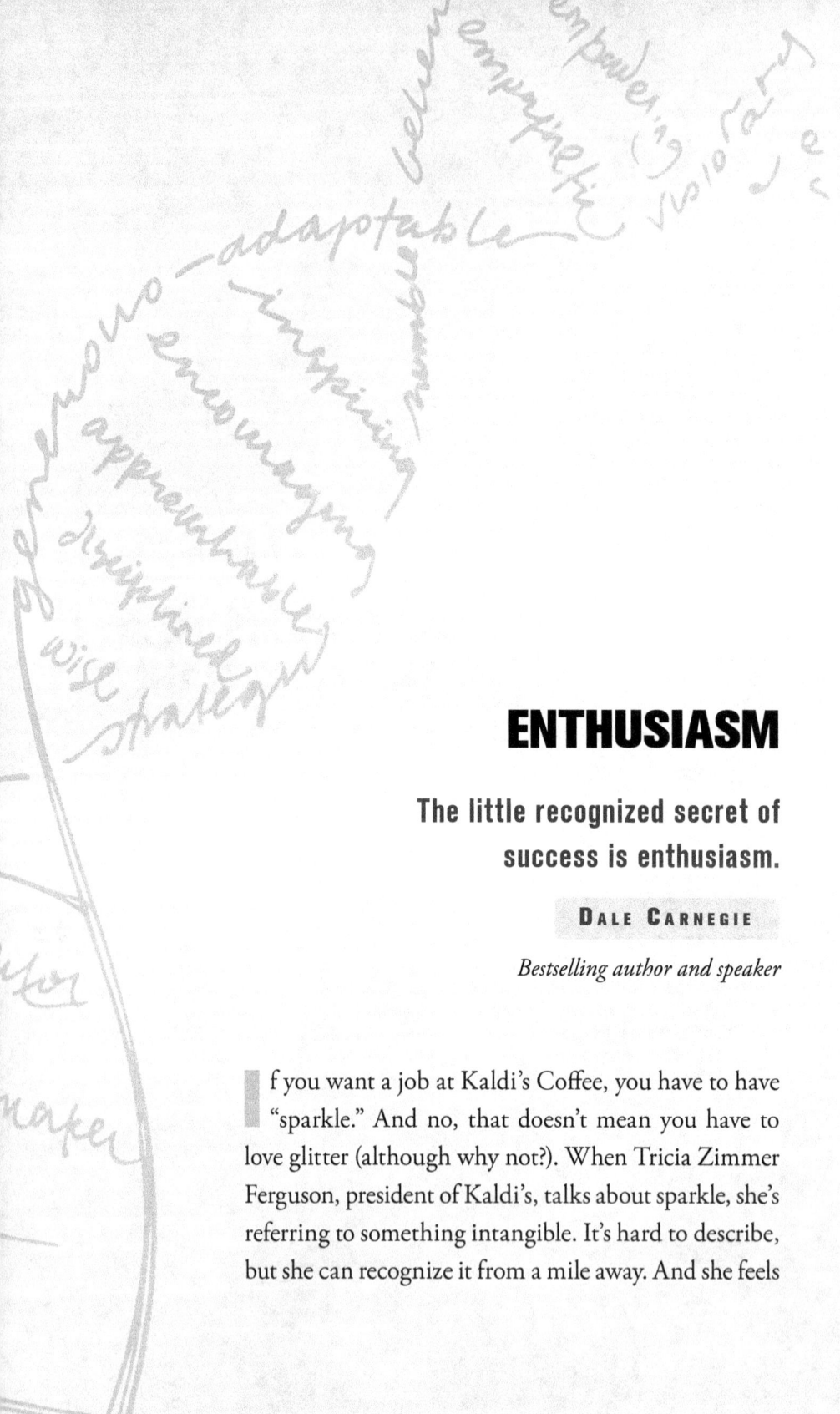

ENTHUSIASM

The little recognized secret of success is enthusiasm.

DALE CARNEGIE

Bestselling author and speaker

f you want a job at Kaldi's Coffee, you have to have "sparkle." And no, that doesn't mean you have to love glitter (although why not?). When Tricia Zimmer Ferguson, president of Kaldi's, talks about sparkle, she's referring to something intangible. It's hard to describe, but she can recognize it from a mile away. And she feels so strongly about sparkle that she added it to the list of attributes she looks for in new team members.

Coffee is Kaldi's product, but Tricia says they're really in the people business. The focus on people includes the customers they serve at Kaldi's and their other brands, including Frothy Monkey, Honolulu Coffee, and Firepot Tea, as well as the many part-time team members who serve their multiple locations.

Training and recruiting are important to any business, but especially Kaldi's. The decentralized structure that comes with multiple locations and many employees requires strong communication and a shared commitment to the company's mission to deliver both high-quality coffee and memorable customer experiences.

Kaldi's invests significant time and effort in hiring, training, and retaining employees who align with its core values. Tricia says they're always trying to keep the pipeline going because you never know when the next all-star is going to walk through the door.

As they train and coach next-level leaders and interview potential new team members, they keep their favorite acronym in mind. Whether it's a high-level leader position or someone working part-time in one of the cafés, Kaldi's team members need to have GIFTS.

- Goal-oriented
- Improvement-oriented
- Fits within the culture
- Track record of success
- Sparkle

The first four are pretty self-explanatory and what you might see at many other companies. But what about sparkle, that intangible thing that ignites passion and enthusiasm in people? Tricia says that's not something you can train. People either have it or they don't. Tricia's dad always told her that you can't make people be passionate; they have to do that for themselves. And now, Tricia sees it every day.

Self-motivated team members with sparkle will take advantage of opportunities the company offers to help them reach their full potential, and they'll go the extra mile to create exceptional experiences for customers.

Tricia says you can't make anyone love coffee, and you only get one chance to wow a guest. Within a couple of minutes of walking through the door, customers can feel the difference. The Kaldi's team is really excited to be there. They aren't just putting in the time. The coffee is good, and the sparkle is contagious.

A GOOD DAY

When I think about enthusiasm and a positive outlook on life, my mind immediately goes to Ally. She definitely has "sparkle."

Ally approaches almost every day and every opportunity with enthusiasm and positivity. A few months ago, she attended a birthday party for a couple of her young girlfriends. It was a bowling party, and mind you, Ally isn't on a bowling team, but that didn't stop her. She threw several spares and even a few strikes. And after every frame, whether she knocked down two pins or all ten, she celebrated by breaking into a little dance. During her friends' turns, she did the same thing, giving them high-fives and enthusiastic praise.

Even on the most ordinary days when nothing particularly special has happened, Ally will look at me and say, "It has been a good day!"

Every time, I think to myself, *Wow! Wouldn't the world be a much better place if we all embraced life with that kind of joy, gratitude, and enthusiasm?*

We need more sparkle in the world. Don't you agree?

BRING THE JUICE

Donnie Campbell is a math teacher and basketball coach in Kansas. Jason Sudeikis, actor and creator of the hit show *Ted Lasso*, played for him. So not coincidentally, Donnie was an inspiration for Jason to create the character of Ted, an American football coach hired to manage a British soccer team. What Ted lacks in the knowledge of soccer, he makes up for in optimism and determination.

Unlike Ted, Donnie's sport is basketball, and his three-plus decades of experience have given him plenty of knowledge. But, like Ted, Donnie believes in the power of positivity, connection, and belief. His story is another powerful perspective on the transformative power of enthusiasm.

Donnie says he doesn't coach basketball; he coaches attitude. "Playing basketball is what you do, but it's not who you are," he often tells his players. His coaching style emphasizes character development over wins, teaching his team the importance of perseverance, trust, and positive energy. For Donnie, enthusiasm isn't about bouncing off the walls; it's about showing up fully engaged and giving 100 percent effort.

The same is true in the classroom. Enthusiasm is one of Donnie's secrets to success. He tells his students, "I can promise this much. I'll come every day with the juice. I need you to do the same." Once he explains he's not talking about orange or apple juice, he goes on to explain that nothing worthwhile was ever achieved without enthusiasm.

And he points out to his students that their level of enthusiasm has a direct impact on those around them. They can be either energy givers or energy vampires. Just like sparkle, the juice is contagious.

LEAD WITH PASSION

Enthusiasm is more than just a personality trait; it's a strategic advantage. Whether you're pouring the perfect latte, coaching a high school basketball team, or celebrating in the bowling alley, passion has a ripple effect. A barista's genuine excitement about coffee can brighten a customer's day and foster long-term loyalty. A coach's unwavering belief in a player can influence not just a game but a lifetime of choices. And Ally's enthusiasm brightens the room for all who encounter her.

Enthusiastic, passionate leaders inspire enthusiastic, passionate teams. And those teams, in turn, create transformational experiences for customers, communities, and the next generation of leaders.

Reflection:

1. Recall a time when you or someone you know displayed true enthusiasm, whether in work, relationships, or a personal pursuit. How did it impact those around you?

2. When have you encountered someone whose enthusiasm was contagious? What qualities made their passion stand out? How did it influence your own mindset or actions?

3. In your daily life or work, how do you bring enthusiasm (your own version of "sparkle" or "juice")? If you don't, what's holding you back?

4. Would you describe yourself as someone who adds energy to a room or someone who drains it? How do you think your level of enthusiasm influences the people you interact with? Dr. Richard Blackaby asks it this way: "Does the joy meter go up when you walk *into* the room . . . or when you walk *out* of the room?"

5. Enthusiasm requires energy. What habits, routines, or practices help you stay energized and avoid burnout so you can consistently bring positive energy to what you do?

 **Action:**

....

Reframe Challenges: When faced with a difficult task, practice shifting your mindset by asking, "How can I bring enthusiasm to this situation?" Then find ways to make it engaging. Use this chart to help shift your mindset.

TASK	WHY DOES IT FEEL DIFFICULT?	HOW CAN I BRING ENTHUSIASM?
Ex. Walking the dog when it rains	I get upset when I am drenched for a mundane task.	I can wear rain boots and bring some childlike energy when jumping in puddles with my dog.

Energy: For the next twenty-four hours, log your activities and interactions, rating them as Draining or Energizing on the number scale. The more draining the activity felt, circle a number closer to 0. The more energizing the activity felt, circle a number closer to 10. Identify trends and adjust accordingly to bring more energy-giving elements into your life.

Activity or Interaction:

DRAINING 0 1 2 3 4 5 6 7 8 9 10 **ENERGIZING**

Activity or Interaction:

DRAINING 0 1 2 3 4 5 6 7 8 9 10 **ENERGIZING**

Activity or Interaction:

DRAINING 0 1 2 3 4 5 6 7 8 9 10 **ENERGIZING**

Activity or Interaction:

DRAINING 0 1 2 3 4 5 6 7 8 9 10 **ENERGIZING**

Activity or Interaction:

DRAINING 0 1 2 3 4 5 6 7 8 9 10 **ENERGIZING**

 **Connection:**

Coffee Chat: Invite a close friend, coworker, or family member to coffee to have a talk about your enthusiasm. Ask them how they perceive your energy. Do you uplift and inspire them? Are there areas where you could bring more enthusiasm? Use their feedback to adjust your enthusiasm level.

Growth:

Enthusiasm Mantra: Create a personal mantra that reinforces your commitment to enthusiasm (e.g., "I bring energy and passion to everything I do." "I have sparkle, and I bring the juice!"). Write it on a sticky note and post it where you'll see it daily.

Morning Energy Ritual: Develop a personal routine that sets the tone for enthusiasm each day (e.g., gratitude practice, listening to energizing music, setting an intention for the day).

 Ally's Something Extra

My mother was always one for a little flair. She had great jewelry, stylish clothes, and tons of shoes, and she always wore fresh-smelling perfume. Following in her Nana's footsteps, Ally got really interested in perfume a few years ago. Any time we were in a department store, she would stop and smell all the testers. She eventually landed on a favorite—Happy by Clinique.

It really is the perfect perfume for her because she is happy 99 percent of the time. In fact, I'd say she's not just happy, she's filled with joy. Her enthusiastic nature means that more often than not she sees the glass half full. I don't mean to say that she never gets disappointed. She certainly does, but she never lets life's circumstances steal her passion.

Ally is quite self-sufficient. She gets herself ready in the mornings and often gives me a report. "I'm ready, Mom. I brushed my teeth. I put my deodorant on. And I have my Happy on."

I always giggle to myself when she says this. It's so simple yet so profound. How we live is a choice. We can grumble our way through the day or we can enthusiastically embrace all that life has to offer.

Do *you* have your Happy on?

 Something Extra Podcast
· ·

► Tricia Zimmer Ferguson, episode 51
► Donnie Campbell, episode 273

CURIOSITY

When you stop learning, you stop leading.

CHERYL BACHELDER

Former CEO of Popeyes

Like many teenagers, Dan Clark enjoyed hanging out with his friends and playing video games. When one of those friends started building websites, Dan was fascinated. What was this cool new technology he could learn? He started asking questions, experimenting with coding, and spending hours trying to figure things out on his own.

He didn't realize it then, but that spark of curiosity about new technology would change the trajectory of his life. What started as a simple interest quickly turned into more. He began building websites for local businesses, starting with the martial arts studio he attended. He created the studio's first website, and it went from getting twenty to thirty leads a month to 100 to 130 leads a month.

Word spread, and Dan began making websites for other martial arts studios. Before long, he was nineteen years old, the owner of his own business, and responsible for lead generation for more than thirty martial arts schools. *Wow!* he thought. *I'm onto something here.*

Dan's path wasn't a traditional one. He dropped out of high school in his senior year and never earned a college degree. His curiosity became his greatest teacher. He kept learning, asking questions, and pushing himself to explore new ideas. He ended up selling the business when he was still young, traveling the world for a bit, and then optimizing how he could help companies use technology to grow.

A near-death experience made Dan realize that though he had done pretty well for himself financially, he really wanted to use technology to do something that truly mattered—something that could make a difference in people's lives.

Around that time, he came across Brain.fm, a company that uses neuroscience-backed music to improve focus, relaxation, and sleep. Dan had always had a hard time focusing. In fact, that's one of the reasons he dropped out of high school. Between diet and technology, he was always looking for different things to help him achieve better concentration and a normal working life. He used to work from ten o'clock at night until four o'clock in the morning four days a week. It was almost as if his brain wouldn't really turn on until around one o'clock in the morning and with two cups of coffee.

Dan gave Brain.fm a try and was blown away—so blown away that he was skeptical and tried to break it. He'd stay up all night and use it. He'd wake up at ten o'clock in the morning and use it. He consistently found himself being able to get into a flow state with the help of the Brain.fm playlists. For the first time in his life, he started waking up at nine o'clock in the morning to work. Within the first several weeks, Brain.fm changed his life.

And it sparked his curiosity. How might this technology transform the world by helping people be their best selves? He reached out to the company founders and offered his services— even for free, if necessary. He was convinced that they were going to change people's lives, and he wanted to be part of it. Today, not only does he work for Brain.fm but he's also the owner and CEO.

What fascinates me about Dan's story is that he never had a perfect plan. He never set out to become a tech entrepreneur or the CEO of a neuroscience-driven company. But his curiosity kept opening doors. He wasn't afraid to explore new paths, to ask "What if?" and to follow that question wherever it led. His success wasn't the result of knowing all the answers in advance; it was the result of his willingness to keep searching for them.

At least once a week, he still asks himself, *What am I curious about? And how can I get better?*

THE POWER OF A CURIOUS MIND

Curiosity is a trait we often associate with children who ask "why" a hundred times a day. But for leaders, entrepreneurs, and innovators, curiosity is so much more than that. It's the driving force behind discovery, growth, and transformation.

Cary Granat, the film producer behind *The Chronicles of Narnia*, *Holes*, *Charlotte's Web*, and other family entertainment, has built his entire career on curiosity. Growing up, he was fortunate to be in a family that encouraged curiosity rather than shutting it down. From a very young age, it was instilled in him that there is always more to learn and that curiosity is a skill that can be developed. That mindset shaped his approach to storytelling, leadership, and business.

Cary doesn't just make films; he studies human behavior, cultural shifts, and audience psychology. He approaches filmmaking the way an anthropologist or sociologist would, always seeking to understand the deeper motivations behind why people connect with certain stories. His goal isn't just to follow trends but to anticipate what audiences will respond to before they even realize it.

I love Cary's approach to curiosity because it's so intentional. He doesn't just stumble upon new ideas; he goes looking for them. He suggests starting every morning by asking ten unanswered questions and ending every night with ten more as a practice to stay engaged, always searching, and never settling for surface-level understanding.

When Cary and his wife began having kids, he realized all over again the power of media and felt a strong conviction that it should be used to instill positive values. In 2000, he made the difficult decision to leave an extremely successful multi-billion-dollar media company that had produced a number of successful films to create a company called Walden. His intended audience was the family—specifically middle-school-aged kids—and his goal was to create entertainment that would recapture the imagination and become a catalyst for curiosity.

CURIOSITY AND INNOVATION

One of the biggest misconceptions about curiosity is that it's something you either have or don't have. But in reality, curiosity is a muscle that can be strengthened. Like Cary's daily questioning practice, curiosity thrives when we make it a habit.

I've seen this play out in my own life. Some of the biggest breakthroughs I've had in business, in leadership, and even in my personal growth have come from moments when I allowed myself to be curious—when I asked "What if?" instead of assuming I already had the answer. I've learned that the leaders who make the greatest impact aren't necessarily the ones with the most experience or expertise; they're the ones who are always learning. And that requires humility—the willingness to admit that we don't know everything and the openness to keep asking questions.

Dan Clark and Cary Granat took different paths, but both built their careers on the same foundation: curiosity. They allowed their questions to guide them toward opportunities they never could have planned for.

I truly believe that curiosity is the key to innovation. When we stop asking questions, we stop growing. And when leaders stop growing, so do their organizations. That's why it's so important to cultivate a culture of curiosity, not just for ourselves but for the people we lead.

The best ideas, the boldest innovations, and the most meaningful progress all come from those who are willing to ask, "What if?"

Reflection:

1. When you seek answers, do you try to affirm what you already believe, or do you like to discover something new?

2. Describe a curious person. Do you use words like *unfocused*, *wandering*, and *distracted* or words like *intrigued*, *open*, and *educated*?

3. Have you ever avoided being curious because it might lead to an uncomfortable truth?

4. What are you most curious about right now?

5. What belief could your curiosity challenge or expand?

 **Action:**

. . . .

Question Tracker: Log new questions you ask each day, focusing on small and big topics. They can be personal, professional, or random curiosities you have. Some examples have been provided for you.

DATE	QUESTION ASKED	FOLLOWED UP? (YES OR NO)	INSIGHTS AND NOTES
3/5/2025	How can I improve my focus without caffeine?	Yes	Discovered techniques of hydration jug
3/6/2025	How can I ask better questions at meetings?	No	Need to find a book on this topic

DATE	QUESTION ASKED	FOLLOWED UP? (YES OR NO)	INSIGHTS AND NOTES

Question-a-Day Practice: Commit to asking one deep, curiosity-driven question every day for a month, focusing on different areas of life.

 ## Connection:

Cross-Interest Groups: Build a community group where members share interests and curiosities from different fields. As a group, set up a calendar to explore each member's topic. This can look like a biweekly meeting presentation, a group outing, or an expert invited to a group dinner to share knowledge. Once each group member has taken a deep dive into their curiosity, start another round of questions.

Curiosity Postcard: Send postcards with a thought-provoking question to friends, family, or colleagues. Invite them to respond and reflect with a letter or postcard back.

 ## Growth:

Learning Sprints: For a quarter of the year, dedicate a week each month to intensely explore a new area of curiosity, recording what you learn and how it changes your perspective.

MONTH	NEW AREA OF CURIOSITY TO EXPLORE
January	
February	
March	

Curiosity Playlist: Create a playlist of TED Talks, podcasts, or audiobooks that feed your curiosity in different areas, and track your reflections.

 ### Something Extra Podcast

- ▶ Cheryl Bachelder, episode 3
- ▶ Dan Clark, episode 149
- ▶ Cary Granat, episode 242

COURAGE

I learned that courage was not the absence of fear, but the triumph over it.

—NELSON MANDELA

Anti-apartheid leader and Nobel Peace Prize laureate

M argie Warrell stood in the airport clutching a bundle of traveler's checks and a one-way ticket out of Australia. At twenty-one years old, she had never been on a plane before. She had no mobile phone, no GPS, and no clear plan beyond the belief that there was more to life than the small dairy farm where she grew up. That leap into the unknown—solo backpacking around the world for a year—became one of the defining experiences of her life.

It taught her self-reliance and how to manage her well-being, finances, and safety. She learned how to read people, trust her instincts, and navigate situations that were often completely foreign to her. From staying in cheap hostels to meeting people who would become lifelong friends, Margie built a foundation of courage she would rely on for the rest of her life. Being thrust out of her comfort zone time and time again while learning and exploring made her realize she was capable of more than she had thought.

Years later, as she stared at the first draft of her book *Find Your Courage*, the fear of the unknown crept in. The voice in her head told her she wasn't qualified, that she didn't belong in the company of published authors. *Who do you think you are? You don't even know where the apostrophes go. How could you aspire to write a book?*

But Margie had learned a thing or two about courage over the years. At the top of the list was the truth that courage is built by doing. She had to push through the doubt, muster her belief in herself, and give herself permission to put her message on paper even if it wasn't perfect.

Today, in addition to being known as a global authority on courageous leadership and human potential, she is also a five-time bestselling author. None of that would have happened if she had let fear have the upper hand.

REFRAMING FEAR

Courage isn't the absence of fear. In fact, Margie says that fear serves a purpose and that being fearless should never be our goal.

Fearless and courageous are not synonyms. Courage is the decision to take action—to risk an unknown outcome—despite fear.

We don't need to completely eradicate fear, but we need to discern when it is serving us and when it is stifling us. Fear comes in many forms, and it's often disguised as mild-mannered self-doubt. *I don't know if I'm experienced enough. I don't know if I have what it takes. I could make a fool of myself. I could be rejected.*

Often, that self-doubt keeps us from taking the very actions that we are wholly capable of such as making a bold ask, taking on a bigger role, or having a difficult conversation. Many people never reach their full potential because fear keeps them playing small. There's a large gap between the life they live and the life they *could* be living. It takes courage to close that gap.

There have been many moments throughout my life and career when I had to choose courage in the face of uncertainty. For me, the only reason I can be courageous is that my belief system is firmly rooted in a power far greater than myself. Greg and I have always drawn strength from Proverbs 3:5–6: "Trust in the LORD with all your heart and lean not on your own understanding; in all your ways submit to him, and he will make your paths straight."

Our faith reminds us that we are never alone. No matter how unclear the path may seem, we trust that God is always with us, guiding our steps. Just as Moses assured the Israelites that "The LORD will fight for you; you need only to be still" (Exodus 14:14), we have clung to that same promise. Even when the way forward was uncertain, we believed that God was making a way.

One defining moment was in 1994 when Greg and I made the decision to start Technology Partners. There were no entrepreneurial boot camps, no step-by-step playbooks, and no mentors walking us through the process. And we certainly didn't have a safety net.

What we did have was a deep belief in our vision, an unwavering trust in God and in each other, and a willingness to take risks. We leaned on our faith, our work ethic, and the lessons we had learned through our ten years in corporate America. Every challenge, every setback, and every unknown only strengthened our resolve.

Looking back, that leap of faith in 1994 was one of the most courageous decisions we ever made. It shaped not just our business but the countless relationships, opportunities, and blessings that have come from it over the past thirty years. And through it all, this one truth has remained: God is faithful. He has guided our every step, and we wouldn't trade this journey for anything.

THE COST OF PLAYING IT SAFE

Fear is real, but it's often not entirely rational. Fear easily creates a distorted perception of risk that almost always skews negative. Rather than focus on our fear, what if we thought about the price we might pay if we *don't* take the brave action? What about the risk of *inaction*?

Courage helps us manage the risks even in the presence of uncertainty. Courage helps us consider the opportunity cost of inaction—missed connections, lost opportunities, and untapped potential. If we don't step out in courage and follow our calling, we are going to miss out, and so is the world.

When we are courageous, we learn, grow, and expand who we are as humans. When we stick with the safety and familiarity of the status quo, we just stay stuck. As Margie says, "Fortune favors the brave."

Not every brave thing we do lands perfectly. Sometimes, things don't work out. We don't get the result we want. That's part of taking courageous action. Rather than view it as a failure, we can view it as a learning experience. I love how Margie says it: "Find your treasure when you trip." Even if things don't go according to plan, there's always something we can learn. And every experience—positive or negative—can empower us to greater bravery next time.

Courage isn't about waiting until we feel ready; it's about moving forward despite uncertainty. If we wait to feel ready before we speak up, step out, or take that next leap, we might be waiting forever. We've all faced our own moments of hesitation, standing on the edge of something new, wondering if we have what it takes.

The only way to build courage is to step forward. Courage comes in the doing. At the end of life, it's the risks we didn't take—the times we weren't brave—that we most often regret.

LEAD WITH PURPOSE

Fear causes us to focus on what we *don't* want—failure, rejection, uncertainty—rather than letting us set our sights on the highest and best vision of our future. Unless we are really clear on what we most *want*, fear will very easily dictate our decisions and direct our lives.

True courage begins with clarity. What do you want? What kind of leader, colleague, or person do you aspire to be?

Margie says that when we're rooted in our deepest values and connected to the highest and holiest vision for our lives, it makes courage easier. It's not necessarily *easy*, but the actions we need to take become clearer. Fear will always exist. It is wired into us for safety and self-preservation. But when we are committed to something bigger than our fear, we unlock an inner strength that propels us forward.

Leaders who stand firm in their principles are better equipped to make difficult decisions. The right path is rarely the easiest or most comfortable one, but when guided by purpose, we find the resolve to step up despite uncertainty. Aristotle said that courage is the foundation for all other virtues. Margie Warrell calls it the *force multiplier* for living our biggest, bravest, and most authentic lives.

In today's volatile world where unpredictability and disruption are the norm, leaders must make bold choices. Those who lead with courage create environments that foster learning, innovation, and candid conversations that serve not just their organizations but everyone around them.

Courage is not just about grand acts of bravery. It's also about everyday choices to speak up, to take a risk, to lead with integrity. Whether it's stepping into a leadership role, advocating for a cause, or simply finding your voice, courage is a leadership muscle that grows with practice.

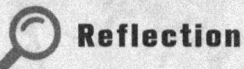

Reflection:

....

1. Looking back on your life, describe a time you had to muster courage despite fear or self-doubt.

2. Who is someone in your life that has demonstrated remarkable courage? How did witnessing their bravery influence your own approach to fear and risk-taking?

3. What risks do you regret not taking in the past?

4. Where in your life are you currently playing it safe instead of stepping into something bigger? What beliefs about yourself might be limiting your ability to act with courage?

5. What's one courageous goal you want to pursue in the next year?

 **Action:**

Fear vs. Reality Chart: Make two columns—one for a fear that's holding you back and one for the realistic outcome if you face it. This helps separate imagined fears from actual risks.

FEAR THAT HOLDS YOU BACK	REALISTIC OUTCOME IF YOU FACE IT
Ex. I want to sell some pottery pieces I made, but I'm afraid no one will like them.	*By offering my pieces for sale, I will learn more about the preferences of my target market.*

Courage Tracker: Write down one courageous action you can take each day for the next seven days, no matter how small. Reflect on what you felt before, during, and after.

Day 1:

Day 2:

Day 3:

Day 4:

Day 5:

Day 6:

Day 7:

 **Connection:**

Courageous Conversations Challenge: Identify a difficult conversation you've been avoiding (personal, professional, or community-related). Maybe it's about a performance improvement plan or something someone said that's made you uncomfortable. Gather your courage and commit to having the difficult conversation this week.

 Growth:

Courageous Identity Statement: Write a personal affirmation that embodies the courageous person you want to be. Example: *I am someone who takes bold action despite uncertainty.* Repeat it daily as a reminder of your growing courage.

I am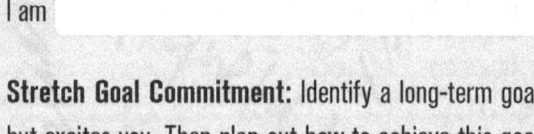

Stretch Goal Commitment: Identify a long-term goal that scares you but excites you. Then plan out how to achieve this goal using this step-by-step outline:

What is your bold, exciting goal?

Why does this goal matter to you?

Who will help hold you accountable?

Step 1: First small action you can take today:

Step 2: Next step within a week:

Step 3: Milestone to hit within a month:

Step 4: Larger step that moves you significantly forward:

Step 5: Final stretch toward goal completion:

Final goal completion date:

Ally's Something Extra

Ally practices being courageous. I have so many funny stories about how she settles herself before an interview or a dance show. I distinctly remember how several years ago she used breathwork to ground herself and slow down her breathing before the camera started rolling.

In 2019, Ally competed in *Dancing with the St. Louis Stars* to benefit the STL Independence Center. Backstage, nerves were running high, even for seasoned executives like Matt Bukhshtaber, vice chairman of CBRE and one of the dancers competing that evening. Later, Matt shared with me how Ally, with her calm and steady presence, walked up to him and said, "Take a deep breath. You've got this."

That simple moment shifted everything. Ally's courage (and encouragement) eased Matt's nerves and brought a sense of calm to all the dancers waiting to take the stage.

Something Extra Podcast

► Dr. Margie Warrell, episodes 219 and 325

RESILIENCE

Resilience is the ability to deal with adversity and still come out passionate and positive.

GINT GRABAUSKAS

Chief Technology Officer at FastGrid

Sean Swarner is the only person in history to have climbed Mount Everest, scaled the highest mountain on each continent, skied to both the North and South Poles, and completed the Hawaii Ironman Triathlon. He holds multiple world records and has been the subject of an Emmy-nominated Amazon film.

But what makes those accomplishments even more astonishing is the fact that Sean is a terminal cancer survivor, spent a year in a medically induced coma, and only has one lung.

Is it any wonder that he is celebrated as one of the top eight most inspirational people in history? I can't write about the topic of resilience without mentioning Sean.

Sean believes we all experience a handful of things that happen that literally change the trajectory of our paths. For him, one of them was being diagnosed at age thirteen—on the cusp of his teen years—with advanced stage four Hodgkin's lymphoma. Doctors gave him only a few months to live. When most kids his age were nervous about who they were going to sit with at lunch in the cafeteria, Sean was worried about waking up the next day. Despite the grim prognosis, he underwent aggressive chemotherapy treatments and ultimately achieved remission.

Unbelievably, just a few years later, he was diagnosed with Askin's tumor, an even rarer and more aggressive cancer. This time doctors only gave him a 6 percent chance of surviving. He underwent surgery to remove one of his lungs and faced another grueling round of treatments. Remarkably, he beat the odds. He survived.

Not only did he survive but he used the trauma to push himself to triumph. Of course he asked himself, *Why me?* But that question had no answer, and he realized that even if it did, it didn't change the facts. So what was he going to do about it? How was he going to live in the situation? How could he live without fear? He decided early on that cancer would not define his life. He shifted his perspective from fear to determination, focusing on what he could control such as his attitude and mental strength.

Sean's life-altering diagnoses, terrible as they were, ended up planting the seeds of resilience, hope, and a deep understanding that challenges can become opportunities for growth.

BUILDING THE RESILIENCE MUSCLE

I don't plan to climb a mountain or complete a triathlon anytime soon, but I do work out three times a week and in the summer walk almost daily with Ally because I know that muscles don't grow unless you use them. The same is true for resilience.

It's almost impossible to build the muscle of resilience without facing and overcoming challenges. It's not easy, but resilience is developed as we respond to adversity. Sometimes that adversity is of our own choosing such as skiing to the North and South Poles, but more often it's something out of our control such as a cancer diagnosis. Things get thrown at us, and dealing with and overcoming hard things are what make us resilient.

One of my favorite visuals is the purification of silver. In this process, the silversmith heats the silver until impurities, or dross, rise to the surface. The dross is then scraped away, and the process is repeated over and over until the silversmith can finally see his reflection in the silver. This is a powerful image of transformation.

Similarly in life, it is through enduring and overcoming difficulties that we are refined, with each trial removing a layer of impurity, shaping us into our truest, most resilient selves. James 1:2–3 captures this beautifully: "Consider it pure joy, my brothers and sisters, whenever you face trials of many kinds, because you know that the testing of your faith produces perseverance." Just like the silversmith's reflection, our own resilience becomes a reflection of our inner strength and growth.

For me, hope and resilience are intertwined. Without hope, resilience falters. Hope can give us the energy we need to push through tough moments. And that is, of course, tied to mindset— choosing hope, maintaining faith, and recognizing setbacks as potential setups for future success.

Sean told me that when he was climbing Mount Everest, he had a running commentary in his head. Each time he lifted his right leg, he told himself, *The higher I go, the stronger I get. The higher I go, the stronger I get.* Sean knew his mind needed to be as strong if not stronger than his body.

He compared his mind to a glass of water. Dirty water represents negative thoughts. Clean water represents positive thoughts. If you have a glass full of dirty water, turn on the faucet, and constantly fill it to overflowing with clean water, eventually you will have a glass of clean water. The same is true for the mind. You can flush out negative thoughts with positive ones and in that way program your brain.

Ultimately, it's our choice how we respond to circumstances, whether we falter or whether we build our resilience muscles.

RISING AFTER A FALL

Bruce Sheridan, EOS Implementer and president of Life Compass, Inc., draws on his personal experiences of overcoming adversity. Bruce grew up in Union, New Jersey, as the fourth of six children in a household affected by poverty and domestic violence. As a toddler, he survived an incident that resulted in serious burns that kept him hospitalized for six weeks. As he grew up, he endured abuse at home and school. At school, he encountered extreme bullying from a group of boys he referred to as the "gang of four." These young men terrorized both students and teachers, once even breaking a teacher's foot. Facing that fear daily took its toll on Bruce.

At home, Bruce endured physical abuse from his father, who had also experienced abuse as a child. As Bruce grew older and physically stronger, he stood up to his father, ending the cycle of violence in their household.

The weight of those experiences led Bruce to attempt suicide at age thirteen, and he later developed substance abuse issues in his young adulthood. Eventually, Bruce made a life-changing commitment to his faith and sought out therapy, which helped him break destructive patterns.

Those early life experiences taught him the importance of resilience, a theme he returns to often. Adversity, while painful, is what helped shape his strength and sense of purpose. Bruce has a passion for mentoring young people and advocating for resilience as a core leadership quality.

Whether during his childhood or as an adult, Bruce knows what it's like to dust himself off and keep going. Yes, sometimes you need to take some time to regroup and recharge, he says, but always get back up and move ahead.

Bruce told me about the day he was suddenly let go from Bank of America. He had built a successful career and worked his way up to a prestigious role, but in a matter of moments that all changed, and he was out of a job. He recalls the day he had to clear out his desk and carry his boxes to the lobby. Some coworkers looked the other way in avoidance while others gave him condolences. It was humiliating and not something he had ever imagined would be part of his story. And what would come next?

It's a scenario many of us fear—losing not just a job but with it a sense of identity and purpose. But Bruce didn't stay down for long. He got back up. And that's the essence of resilience. Acknowledge the hurt and disappointment but refuse to let it define you.

As leaders, we often focus on strategy, skills, and vision. But none of those matter if we don't have the resilience to weather the storms. Leadership isn't about having all the answers or avoiding failure. It's about showing up, even when things get tough. It's about leading with courage, humility, and a willingness to learn from every experience. It's the ability to face life's hardest moments, dig deeply, and come out stronger, wiser, and more compassionate on the other side.

 **Reflection:**

1. Looking back on your life, what is one significant challenge that tested your resilience? How did you respond? What did you learn about yourself in the process?

2. When have you witnessed someone display extraordinary resilience in the face of adversity? How did their response impact you?

3. In your current life situation, where do you see an opportunity to strengthen your resilience? What obstacles are you facing that could ultimately help refine your character and inner strength?

4. How do you typically respond to setbacks or failures? Do you find yourself dwelling on difficulties, or are you able to shift your mindset toward growth and perseverance?

5. What habits, mindsets, or support systems can you cultivate now to help you stay strong in difficult times?

 Action:

Your Self-Talk: Think of a challenge you've had this week or this month. Take note of your self-talk during that difficult moment. Keep track of negative versus positive thoughts and consciously work on reframing setbacks as opportunities to grow. List what sort of things you say to yourself in each category below.

POSITIVE THOUGHTS I SAY TO MYSELF	NEGATIVE THOUGHTS I SAY TO MYSELF

Your Victory List: Record below the times you've successfully pushed through a difficult situation this year, no matter how small. Keep this list to serve as proof of your growing resilience.

My wins this year:

1. Ex. Setting a goal to walk a mile every day in January and completing it.
2. _____
3. _____
4. _____
5. _____

 **Connection:**

See It for Yourself: Seek out a cause in your community that supports individuals facing hardship. It might be mentoring at-risk youth or working with a support group. Ask to visit and volunteer or observe for one day. Notice how resilience plays a role in their lives and how you can apply those lessons to your own challenges.

Lift Someone Up: Make a list of five people in your life who you care about and highlight anyone who might be going through a challenge right now. Write down one way you can support that person in their resilience journey. Take action to encourage or uplift them this week.

IMPORTANT PERSON IN YOUR LIFE	CHECK IF THEY NEED SUPPORT	IDEAS TO LIFT UP THEIR RESILIENCE
1.		
2.		
3.		
4.		
5.		

Growth:

Personal Resilience Challenge: Pick an area where you often struggle (handling criticism, pushing through setbacks, staying patient) and commit to practicing a new, stronger response over the next month.

Your Resilience Reminder: Choose a quote, mantra, or memory of a past triumph. Write it down on a sticky note and stick it on your mirror or the fridge door so you can see it every day. Keep it visible for when you need motivation during tough times.

Get Out of Your Comfort Zone: Identify a comfort zone you tend to stay in and intentionally push past it. Whether it's public speaking, starting a difficult conversation, or tackling a big goal, reflect on how stepping into discomfort strengthens resilience.

 ## Something Extra Podcast

► Bruce Sheridan, episode 229
► Gint Grabauskas, episode 288
► Sean Swarner, episode 307

ADAPTABILITY

If I had a dime for every time I had to learn a different way to do something, I'd be rich.

CHRIS LUNDEBERG

Chief Solutions Architect at Technology Partners

magine being 400 nautical miles offshore, alone in a tiny vessel, the vast ocean stretching endlessly in every direction. The waves crash harder than expected, the wind shifts unpredictably, and the plan you so meticulously crafted no longer applies. In that moment, you have two choices: resist the change, fight against forces beyond your control, or adapt by adjusting your strategy, shifting your mindset, and navigating forward.

Those were the options facing ocean navigator, explorer, and adventurer Cyril Derreumaux in 2022 on his second attempt to solo kayak across the Pacific from California to Hawaii.

Alone in his kayak (named *Valentine* after his sister), Cyril had already been on the water for nearly a month. He'd had problems with multiple systems on his boat—steering lines, batteries, and other mechanical issues—and he had to make a decision.

He could return to Los Angeles, which would take a week and mean giving up the 400 miles he'd already covered. He could analyze what went wrong, fix his kayak, and attempt the crossing at a later date. Or he could commit fully and proceed ahead to Hawaii—another 2,000 nautical miles and two months' time. He would have to fix anything that broke along the way, on his own in the middle of the ocean.

The choice to continue was not just about endurance; it was about committing fully to the unknown in spite of his doubt and uncertainty. Cyril ultimately chose to press forward, calling this moment his "second departure." Leaving the pier in California was one thing, but this was his *all-in* moment. He determined that he would "adapt and adapt and adapt."

Chances are that your circumstances are quite different from Cyril's. I know that I don't plan to kayak to Hawaii anytime soon. But his story mirrors the reality of many of us in leadership. Our ability to adapt is often the difference between metaphorically sinking or sailing forward.

The world is moving faster than ever. Market trends shift overnight, technology evolves in the blink of an eye, and global events reshape entire industries. As leaders (and even as human beings simply existing in the world), we cannot rely on rigid plans or past successes. We must embrace adaptability as a skill and a mindset that allows us to lead through uncertain times.

ADAPTABILITY IN LEADERSHIP

Whether leading a team, running a business, or navigating personal growth, the ability to adjust, stay mentally agile, and make decisions in real time separates those who survive from those who thrive. Dr. Richard Blackaby, a leadership expert I deeply respect, says leaders are essentially problem-solvers. And, ultimately, he says, we don't lead organizations or businesses; we lead people.

Richard has spent years studying leadership and working with executives. One of his strongest beliefs is that leaders must adapt their leadership styles based on the individuals they lead. Rigid, one-size-fits-all leadership doesn't work.

Effective leaders, he says, know how to read the room and adjust on the fly. They look at the people they're working with and ask, *What makes this person tick? What tool do I need to pull out of my leadership toolbox to best serve them?*

They adapt. They tweak and adjust until they find what Richard calls the *sweet spot.* Some employees thrive with structure and direct oversight; others excel when given autonomy. Some respond well to encouragement; others need a challenge to stay motivated. And when both leader and team are working in the sweet spot, that's when things get really dynamic.

Effective leadership requires keen observation, thoughtful analysis, and a willingness to adapt. The phrase "the only constant is change" has never been more relevant, especially in technology where advancements can render solutions obsolete in as little as eighteen months. Successful leaders remain attuned to both the shifting landscape and the evolving needs of their teams, adjusting their approach to drive the best possible outcomes.

The most successful leaders I know aren't just problem-solvers; they are problem-embracers. Rather than resisting change, they embrace it, recognizing that flexibility is not a weakness but a strength. They don't panic when a plan unravels. They actively listen and assess challenges with an open mind, asking, "What's my next move?"

In times of uncertainty, teams don't need leaders who cling to outdated processes. They need leaders who foster a culture of innovation, resilience, and continuous learning. Empowering teams to embrace change with confidence requires equipping them with the right mindset and tools to navigate an ever-evolving environment. Ultimately, adaptability in leadership is about striking the right balance between conviction and agility, knowing when to stand firm and when to pivot.

For over thirty years, Technology Partners has thrived by embracing adaptability. Whether it was strategically opening new offices, expanding service lines to meet evolving client needs, or navigating the complexities of a global pandemic, our leadership has consistently risen to the challenge.

Now, as generative AI reshapes industries with an astonishing 42 percent compound annual growth rate, we are once again positioning ourselves at the forefront. We are anticipating change, embracing innovation, and empowering our teams to lead with confidence in an AI-driven world. We are committed to being AI-forward thinkers by investing in continuous learning, upskilling our workforce, and integrating AI-driven solutions into our services.

ADAPTING IN THE MOMENT

Adaptability isn't just about responding to unexpected changes; it's also about how we respond when the unexpected becomes the norm. Jeff Glasbrenner, a three-time Paralympian and an elite Ironman triathlete, knows a thing or two about adapting to a new normal.

As a child, Jeff was told he would never live an active life. He lost his leg in a farming accident at age eight, and doctors gave him a list of things he couldn't do. But Jeff didn't accept those limits. Despite being told he wouldn't be able to run, swim, or participate in sports, he became a three-time Paralympian and a two-time world champion in wheelchair basketball. He has completed twenty-five Ironman races and climbed Mount Everest.

His story is a reminder that adaptability isn't just about reacting to external change; it's also about choosing to see challenges as opportunities rather than roadblocks. Jeff could have let his amputation define him. Instead, he adapted his training, developed new techniques, and rewrote the rules of what was possible.

As an adaptive athlete, Jeff is well acquainted with the fact that life throws curveballs. He tells the story of climbing Mount Vinson in Antarctica when the extreme cold froze and broke a critical part of his prosthetic leg. With no backup parts and no easy way off the mountain, he and his team had to improvise a solution using duct tape and whatever materials they had on hand. Instead of panicking, Jeff did what he had done his entire life. He adapted. He refused to let the setback stop him from reaching the summit.

In leadership, as in mountaineering, the conditions will never be exactly as you imagined. The business climate shifts, employees leave, and market demands change. The best leaders aren't those who stubbornly cling to a single strategy but those who adjust their approach without losing sight of their goal.

Adaptable leaders are flexible and resilient, and they think strategically. One of the best ways to strengthen adaptability is to get comfortable with uncertainty. Expect change. Stay curious by looking ahead. And know yourself so you can respond thoughtfully rather than react impulsively. Like Jeff, learn to focus not on what should have been but on what is.

THE FUTURE BELONGS TO THE ADAPTABLE

If there's one thing I want you to take away from this chapter, it's this: The leaders who thrive in the future will be the ones who embrace adaptability today. Change isn't slowing down. Nobody knows that better than the CEO of a technology company in the twenty-first century.

The unexpected will continue to happen. But that doesn't have to be a bad thing. As leaders, we have a choice. We can resist change, or we can rise to the occasion. The world needs leaders who adapt to change in a way that creates something extraordinary.

And when adaptability becomes second nature, we lead with a sense of peace, knowing we can face whatever comes our way.

Reflection:

1. How do you usually react when plans fall apart? Do you panic, problem-solve, or do something else?

2. When was the last time you had to "just figure it out"? Describe what happened. What did you learn?

3. If you had to make a major change today, what would scare you the most?

4. What's one routine or mindset you could tweak to make yourself more adaptable?

5. If you could give your younger self one piece of advice about handling change, what would it be?

 **Action:**

Flexibility Meter: Rank yourself on a scale of 1 to 10 in different areas of adaptability. After rating yourself, reflect on your strengths and areas for growth.

HANDLING UNEXPECTED CHANGES: 1 2 3 4 5 6 7 8 9 10

- ► 1–3 (Resistant): Change makes you anxious. You struggle to adjust quickly and prefer sticking to plans.
- ► 4–6 (Neutral): You can adapt if needed, but it takes effort and discomfort.
- ► 7–10 (Flexible): You embrace change easily and adjust without much stress.

PROBLEM-SOLVING UNDER PRESSURE: 1 2 3 4 5 6 7 8 9 10

- ► 1–3 (Overwhelmed): You tend to freeze or panic when faced with an unexpected challenge.
- ► 4–6 (Moderate): You work through problems but may need extra time or guidance.
- ► 7–10 (Quick thinker): You thrive under pressure, quickly finding creative solutions.

WILLINGNESS TO TRY NEW THINGS: 1 2 3 4 5 6 7 8 9 10

- ► 1–3 (Resistant): You stick to familiar routines and avoid trying new methods or ideas.
- ► 4–6 (Open but hesitant): You will try something new if necessary, but it's uncomfortable.
- ► 7–10 (Adventurous): You actively seek out new experiences and enjoy learning new approaches.

ADJUSTING IN WORK AND RELATIONSHIPS: 1 2 3 4 5 6 7 8 9 10

- ► 1–3 (Rigid): You struggle with different personalities, changing work environments, or shifting expectations.
- ► 4–6 (Moderate): You can adapt but need time and effort to adjust to others' needs.
- ► 7–10 (Highly adaptable): You read situations well, adjust your approach, and collaborate easily.

Decision Tree: Choose a past challenge and map out a different way you could have adapted.

PAST CHALLENGE	MY ACTUAL RESPONSE	OPTIONAL ADAPTIVE RESPONSE
Ex. My car wouldn't start in the morning.	I called work in a panic and pretended I was sick.	I could have called a rideshare or a friend to drive me if I had problem-solved rather than panicked.

Connection:

Community Change Analysis: Think about a major shift in your local community or workplace. Maybe it was a leadership change or a new policy being implemented. Maybe an old building in your town was torn down so a popular chain restaurant could be built. How did people react? What worked well and what didn't? How did adaptability—or lack of it—play a role?

Growth:

Controlled Disruptions: Intentionally change up a routine (take a different route to work, try a new method for a task) and reflect on how you handle small, unexpected shifts.

Plan a "Disruption Day": Intentionally disrupt your normal routine (take a different route to work, try a new food, rearrange your workspace) and observe how you respond. Reflect on what you learned about your adaptability.

 **Ally's Something Extra**

Ally began taking ballroom dance lessons in August 2018, and by January 2019, she was competing in *Dancing with the Saint Louis Stars*. She won three out of four categories and raised an amazing $160,000 for charity.

As Ally has continued dancing and competing, countless moments have showcased her incredible adaptability. One example I'll never forget happened during a recent holiday performance. In the middle of her routine, her shoe strap suddenly broke. The music stopped. The crowd fell silent. For a moment, I saw her vulnerability, that split second of uncertainty.

But true to who she is, Ally didn't freeze. She adapted with grace and quick thinking. Without missing a beat, she turned to the audience, stretched her arms wide, and began singing "Silent Night." Her beautiful voice filled the room, transforming what could have been an awkward stumble into a magical, unforgettable moment. While her partner quickly fixed her shoe, Ally captivated the crowd with her poise and presence. When the music resumed, she stepped right back into the dance as if nothing had happened—a living example of adaptability in action.

 Something Extra Podcast

- ► Dr. Richard Blackaby, episode 9
- ► Jeff Glasbrenner, episode 134
- ► Chris Lundeberg and Jake Gower, episode 297
- ► Cyril Derreumaux, episode 304

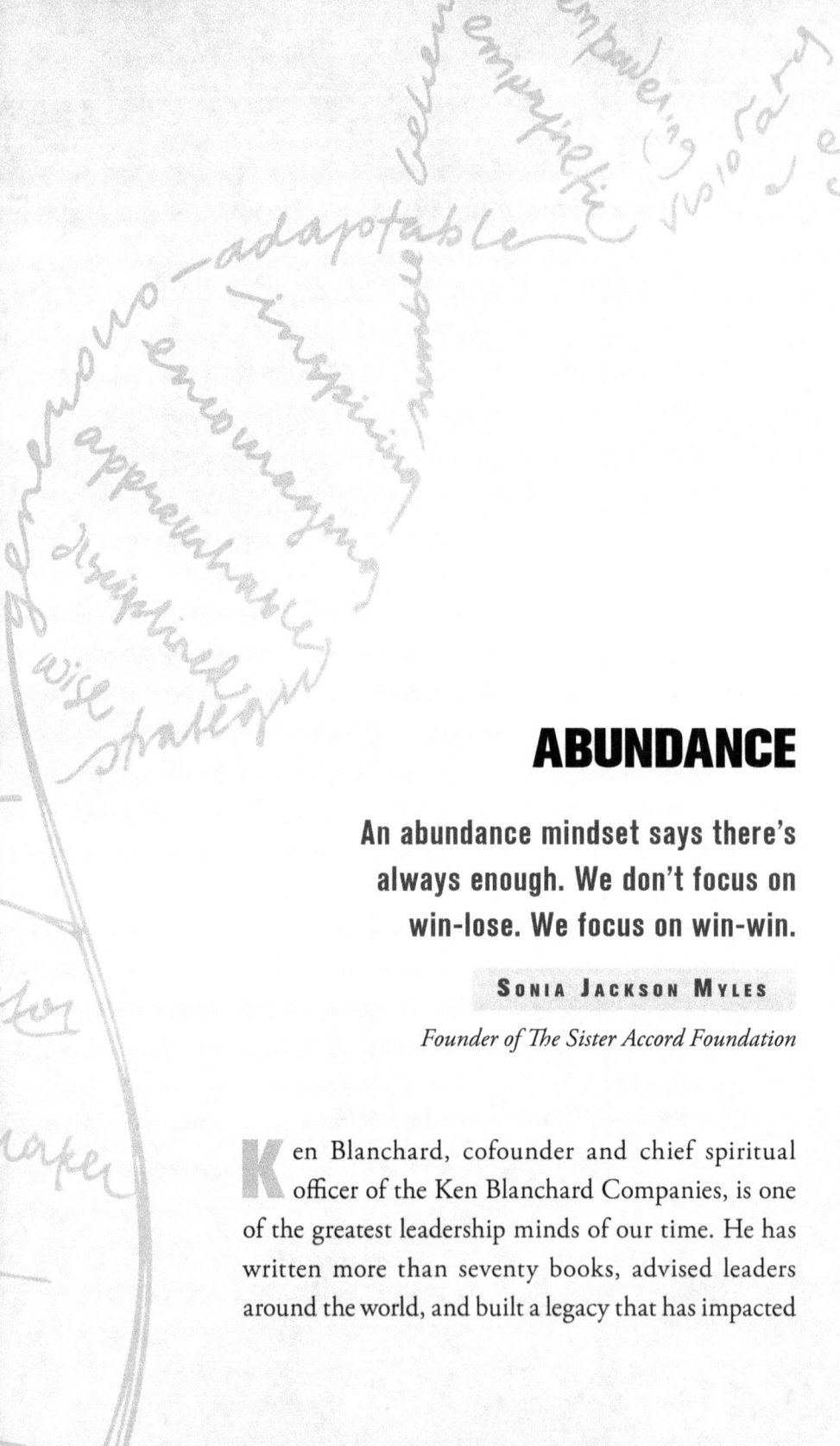

ABUNDANCE

An abundance mindset says there's always enough. We don't focus on win-lose. We focus on win-win.

Sonia Jackson Myles

Founder of The Sister Accord Foundation

Ken Blanchard, cofounder and chief spiritual officer of the Ken Blanchard Companies, is one of the greatest leadership minds of our time. He has written more than seventy books, advised leaders around the world, and built a legacy that has impacted countless individuals. Yet when I asked him about leadership, he didn't talk about power or personal achievement. He didn't focus on his own accolades.

Instead, he said this: "The biggest *something extra* is to get out of your own way and to realize that you're not the center of the universe. You're only as good as the people you gather around you. If you help your people look good, they'll help you look good. And it's a win, win, win."

That statement sums up what I've come to believe about true leadership. It isn't about holding on to power; it's about giving it away. This is the core of an abundance mindset.

Abundance says there is enough success, enough opportunity, and enough impact to go around. When we lead with abundance, we don't hoard knowledge, control, or credit. Instead, we freely invest in others, trusting that success grows when it is shared.

Abundant leaders multiply success, not just for themselves but for the people and organizations they serve.

THE ABUNDANCE PRINCIPLE

If abundance says there's always enough, scarcity says the opposite. Scarcity says we need to compete for what's ours. Competition is not necessarily a bad thing. It has existed since the beginning of time, after all. But competition naturally leads to comparison, and that is where competition can become unhealthy and dangerous.

Unhealthy comparison often stems from a scarcity mindset, especially regarding more senior roles in the marketplace. Leaders with a scarcity mindset believe this:

- Opportunities are limited. If someone else wins, that means you lose.

- Power must be protected. They hoard knowledge, believing that sharing it weakens their influence.

- Success is a zero-sum game. They see leadership as a constant battle for control rather than a platform for service.

I have observed many women struggle with unhealthy comparisons. I imagine the same can be said of men, but I only have a woman's vantage point. I have been there too many times. But as I have conscientiously worked on becoming more comfortable with who I am and how God uniquely wired me, I can honestly say I would rather collaborate and celebrate than compare. As Oscar Wilde famously said, "Be yourself; everyone else is already taken."

I would rather have an abundance mindset that says this:

- There is always more—more success, more opportunities, more ways to grow and contribute.

- Success multiplies when shared. Helping others succeed does not diminish my own success. It expands it.

- Collaboration beats competition. The best leaders mentor, support, and create opportunities for others rather than seeing them as threats.

The possibilities created by collaborating and lifting each other up are so powerful. True success is not a zero-sum game. There is room for all of us to thrive. When we shift from competition to collaboration, we unlock new opportunities, foster deeper relationships, and create impact far beyond what we could achieve alone.

I have found that when I choose to celebrate others rather than compare myself to them, I experience greater joy, fulfillment, and confidence in my own path. We each bring something unique to the table, and the world benefits when we embrace and uplift one another.

So instead of measuring ourselves against someone else's success, let's focus on becoming the best version of ourselves. Let's lead with an abundance mindset, knowing that by lifting others, we all rise.

THE POWER OF RECIPROCITY

Elise Mitchell is a leadership strategist, executive coach, and the founder of Mitchell Communications Group, a firm she grew from a startup to a top-ranked public relations agency before successfully selling it. She is also the author of *Leading Through the Turn*, a book that explores leadership through the lens of navigating change and uncertainty.

Elise and I first connected through a spiritual leadership institute designed by the CEO Forum for high-level female executives. Our relationship was originally structured as a mentorship, and I was to serve as Elise's mentor. But that dynamic soon evolved into a mutual mentorship and now a friendship in which we learn and grow together.

I quickly saw how committed Elise is to the concept of living out of an abundance mindset. In fact, I call her a *go-giver*. Every time I ask for insight on one thing or another, she says, "Oh, I have a resource for that. Let me send it to you." She never holds back.

A scarcity mindset often causes people to resist sharing their knowledge or resources because it seems like they're giving away their power. But Elise believes deeply in the power of reciprocity—freely sharing knowledge, resources, and opportunities with others, knowing that someday it will come back to her. She's always asking, "How can I create benefit for you?"

This philosophy has guided her career, reinforcing the idea that true success comes to the givers, not the takers, as they give without keeping score, share without fearing loss, and trust that generosity creates long-term success.

An abundance mentality builds trust. When you have somebody like Elise in your life who freely gives, you trust them. You know they have your best interest at heart.

When leaders operate with a scarcity mindset, people hold back, compete, and protect themselves. But when leaders operate with abundance, people open up, collaborate, and innovate together.

A LEGACY OF ABUNDANCE

If anyone has built a legacy of abundance, it's Ken Blanchard. Ken told me that the best leaders are those who understand that their power flows through them, not from them, and that effective leaders focus on we, not me.

Ken credits his mom and dad for helping him gain that perspective. They would often tell him, "Now, don't you act like a big deal. You're only as good as the people around you." His mom would go on to say, "Everybody's got that pearl of goodness in them. If you're a digger looking for pearls, you don't have to spend all your time on your own pearls."

Ken looks at all he's been able to accomplish over the years and feels blessed. When we spoke, he was around eighty-three years old and working on another book. After decades of leadership, writing, and mentoring, he remains as energized as ever. He is still embracing life with boundless enthusiasm, determined to live with gusto until his very last day.

That mindset has profoundly impacted me. Now in my sixth decade, I want to embody that same spirit—to wake up each morning with purpose, knowing that as long as God grants me another day, I have an opportunity to make a difference in someone's world.

Ken's legacy isn't just about his books or his achievements; it's about the thousands of leaders he has equipped. That's abundant leadership—creating success, impact, and opportunity beyond yourself. The best leaders aren't focused on their own power; they're focused on empowering others. They believe success multiplies when shared and giving creates more opportunities, not less.

So let me ask you this: How will you lead with abundance today?

As Ken says, the best is not behind you. The best is yet to come.

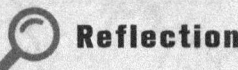 **Reflection:**

1. Think back to times you've been successful. Did you share credit or recognition with others? If so, what motivated you in those moments?

2. How do you typically respond when others experience success, especially in areas you care about deeply?

3. How do you tend to act when you're in a season where resources, time, or energy feel limited?

4. When everything feels like it's going well and you have what you need, how does that influence the way you think, make decisions, or approach life?

5. Who around you could benefit from your mentorship, resources, or encouragement right now?

 Action:

Abundance Self-Assessment: For each of the eight areas below, rank yourself on a scale of 1 to 10 based on how strongly you believe and act from an abundance mindset in that area.

► 1 = Mostly scarcity (protective, withholding, competitive, fear-driven)
► 10 = Fully abundant (generous, collaborative, open, trusting)

Work/Leadership: How freely you share knowledge, create opportunities, and celebrate others in professional spaces.

Rating: 1 2 3 4 5 6 7 8 9 10

Relationships: How open, generous, and trusting you are with the people closest to you.

Rating: 1 2 3 4 5 6 7 8 9 10

Time: How willing you are to give time without guilt or fear of losing control over your schedule.

Rating: 1 2 3 4 5 6 7 8 9 10

Finances: How secure you feel in giving, sharing, or investing without fear of lack.

Rating: 1 2 3 4 5 6 7 8 9 10

Knowledge/Expertise: How freely you share what you know and support others' growth without holding back.

Rating: 1 2 3 4 5 6 7 8 9 10

Opportunities: How strongly you believe that there are enough opportunities for everyone to succeed.

Rating: 1 2 3 4 5 6 7 8 9 10

Recognition/Credit: How comfortable you are giving credit to others and staying grounded without external validation.

Rating: 1 2 3 4 5 6 7 8 9 10

Community/Service: How actively and generously you contribute to causes or people beyond your immediate circles.

Rating: 1 2 3 4 5 6 7 8 9 10

 **Connection:**

Gratitude Without Comparison: List three people in your life who are thriving in some way. Write one sentence about how their success adds value to the world and how their wins don't diminish yours.

NAME AND RELATIONSHIP	THEIR SUCCESS	HOW THEIR SUCCESS ADDS VALUE TO THE WORLD
Ex. Derek, former classmate	*He just published his first book.*	*His voice is adding something meaningful to the world, and just because he's speaking doesn't mean I've lost my chance to speak too.*

 **Growth:**

Give Without Keeping Score: Set a goal to give something away (your time, knowledge, encouragement, or a connection) each week for a month without expecting anything in return.

List your weekly goals:

Week 1:

Week 2:

Week 3:

Week 4:

Abundance Mindset Rewrite: Take a recurring fear or limiting belief you carry and rewrite it into an abundance mindset.

Ex. "There's not enough time."

"I have enough time for what matters most."

Now you try:

Something Extra Podcast

··

- ► Elise Mitchell, episode 96
- ► Sonia Jackson Myles, episode 147
- ► Ken Blanchard, episode 200

LIFELONG LEARNING

**Being a quick learner will give you a
running start, but being a lifelong learner
will take you over the finish line.**

ELISE MITCHELL

Leadership strategist, executive coach, and author

When Maxine Clark was just six years old, she
had one of those teachers you never forget—
the kind who doesn't just teach you how to read or do
arithmetic but teaches you something about life. Her
name was Ms. Grace.

Every Friday, Ms. Grace walked to the front of the classroom with a prize in her hand—a bright red pencil she used for marking her students' papers. Those red pencils were something of a status symbol among Maxine and her classmates. They would open their little cigar box pencil cases cluttered with scissors, glue, and crayons, and compare: *How many red pencils do you have?*

But here's the interesting thing. The red pencil prize didn't go to the student with perfect attendance or the smartest or best-behaved student. Rather it went to the child who had made the most mistakes—the student who had misspelled a word, pronounced something incorrectly, or miscalculated a math sum.

Ms. Grace would smile and say, "Congratulations. You learned the most this week." She wanted her tiny students to learn this big lesson: It's okay to be wrong. It's okay to ask a lot of questions. Mistakes aren't something to hide. They are something to study and grow from.

Mistakes are not a problem if you turn them into learning opportunities.

Can you imagine what that did for Ms. Grace's students? For their confidence? For their courage? For their curiosity? In Maxine's case, those red pencils forever changed the way she thought about learning.

Little Maxine grew up and went on to become a successful entrepreneur and the founder of Build-A-Bear Workshop. Today, she carries a red pencil or two in her purse, always at the ready to hand one to whomever might need to hear that mistakes are not setbacks but springboards. Learning is a lifelong pursuit, not a box we check when we graduate from school, whether it's from Ms. Grace's first-grade classroom or higher education.

BOOKS, PEOPLE, ACTION

Lifelong learning is a topic I am deeply passionate about. From the time I was a little girl, I have had a growth mindset, always believing there was another level to reach. I firmly believe that if we are not learning and growing, we are slipping backward. Learning through reading has always been one of my greatest joys. Give me a cozy chair and a good book, and I am in heaven on earth.

Laura Padousis, executive vice president at Dierbergs Markets, a family-run grocery chain in St. Louis, Missouri, didn't *read* her way into learning to be an executive. She walked it—aisle by aisle in the family store. Her learning of business leadership skills began at age twelve. Laura had watched her older brothers begin to work in the family business, and she wanted to do something too. The employees in the floral department agreed to keep her busy filling little water tubes for the floral arrangements. It was fun. Laura felt like she was adding value, and most of all, she was learning.

Each summer after that, she took on new roles—cashiering, stocking fruit in the produce department, or advising customers in the video center—absorbing knowledge like a sponge. She didn't realize at the time that those little nuggets of learning were all contributing to something she would eventually harness and take into what she does today.

After college, she honored a family rule to work outside the family business first. Then she returned to Dierbergs and completed a full-year rotation across departments. That immersion, she says, gave her not only operational insight but relational understanding— how to lead by knowing what people actually do, not just what's written in their job descriptions.

Laura's dad continued to emphasize learning and improvement

in the family business. Laura jokes about how every family vacation included a trip to see another grocery store. They might be enjoying the beach or some other fun location, and her dad would announce, "Come on, everybody. We're going to go see some grocery stores." He was committed to learning from others, adjusting to new best practices, and bringing ingenuity to Dierbergs.

Like Laura's dad, I also love learning from others. Hosting the *Something Extra* podcast for nearly seven years has only deepened my commitment to lifelong learning. Every guest I have had the honor to interview has enriched my perspective in profound ways.

Several years ago, I had an experience that forever reinforced my belief in the power of learning and growth. Greg and I have been blessed to know Dr. Richard Blackaby, a world-renowned speaker, former seminary president, prolific author, and executive mentor. He has served as a spiritual guide to us through an organization we dearly love, the CEO Forum.

During one of his visits to St. Louis, his team asked me to arrange various speaking engagements for him. Given his influence and wisdom, there was no shortage of eager audiences. I reserved Friday evening for a gathering of young professionals at our recreation barn. As Richard spoke about the importance of lifelong learning, he said something so profound that it has stayed with me ever since.

"When we refuse to grow and learn, someone in our sphere of influence will be hurt," he said. "The people God has entrusted to us deserve for us to be the best version of ourselves."

Wow! That statement shifted my perspective. Our personal growth isn't just about us; it's about those we are called to serve, lead, and guide. Whether it's our children, employees, friends, or communities, everyone around us benefits when we commit to learning and growing. When we show up as our best selves, we all win.

WHAT LIFELONG LEARNERS DO

Someone once asked Tom Ziglar—speaker, author, CEO at Ziglar, Inc., and son of the legendary Zig Ziglar—the secret to Zig Ziglar's success. What made him Zig Ziglar?

Tom pointed to one incredible habit. Every day for five decades, Zig invested the first three hours of his day learning something new—reading God's Word and reading subject matter experts. His motive was to learn, internalize the new information, simplify it, and then share it for someone else's benefit.

Maybe you don't have three hours, but imagine the impact if we set aside just ten minutes a day to do the same—to intentionally learn something new and pass it on to a friend, a colleague, or a family member. Over time, those small, consistent efforts would transform us as well as the people around us. Now picture the difference after a year. After a lifetime. What kind of legacy could we build just by learning something new and sharing it with others as a daily habit?

Learning isn't a season; it's a mindset. It's not something we outgrow; it's something we grow into. Whether it's through a red pencil, a great book, a humbling failure, or a word of wisdom from someone who's been where we're headed, the path of leadership is the path of learning.

The leaders we admire most—the ones who change organizations, shift cultures, and make a lasting impact—aren't the ones who have all the answers. They're the ones who keep asking questions. They see mistakes as a source of innovation. They embed learning into the rhythms of life and work.

So let's be those leaders. Let's show up curious. Let's build teams that get smarter together. And let's never, ever stop learning a little *something extra* every day.

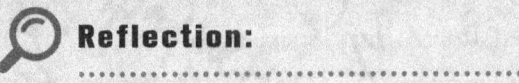 **Reflection:**

1. What's something you used to believe you weren't good at that you've since grown in?

2. What's one mistake you're actually grateful for now because of what it taught you?

3. How do you handle the discomfort of being a beginner at something?

4. Who around you has modeled what it looks like to keep learning, no matter their age or role?

5. What's one thing you'd love to get better at this year? How might you start?

 **Action:**

Red Pencil Scorecard: Just like Maxine Clark's story, reflect and log your biggest weekly mistake and what it taught you. Then celebrate it as your Red Pencil Moment.

MISTAKE OR MISSTEP	WHAT DID I LEARN?	HOW WILL I APPLY THIS?	DID I SHARE IT WITH ANYONE?	RED PENCIL EARNED?
Ex. Forgot to follow up with a client	Systems matter; relying on memory isn't enough	Set reminders and a follow-up checklist	Yes, at the team meeting	✔

Connection:

Team Curiosity Prompts: Consider your work teams, classrooms, or social circles. Ask the members of your group to bring to the next meeting one question they're currently exploring, learning about, or wrestling with. Throughout the next quarter, intentionally ask about their learning journey and create a culture where people feel comfortable sharing their mistakes and successes in something new.

 Growth:

Failure Reframe Statements: List three things you've been hesitant to try because of fear. For each, write a reframe statement about how failing at it could still be a win.

FEAR STATEMENT	REFRAME STATEMENT
Ex. If I speak up in a meeting and my idea isn't well received, I'll look unprepared.	*Even if the idea doesn't land, I'll be practicing courage, clarity, and visibility. I'll also learn how to communicate better next time.*

Three-Month Learning Challenge Activity: Choose one topic, skill, or area of growth. Commit to learning deeply over the next three months through intentional input, experimentation, and reflection.

STEP 1: What do you want to learn, explore, or grow in over the next three months?

Choose one focus area:

- ► Personal
- ► Professional
- ► Physical
- ► Social
- ► Creative

Topic or skill:

Why this matters to me:

STEP 2: Create Your Learning Plan

How will you engage with the topic each month? List the books, podcasts, conversations, online courses, experiments, or mentors you'll tap into.

Month 1:

Month 2:

Month 3:

STEP 3: Monthly Checkpoints

At the end of each month, pause and reflect on what you're learning—not just the content but how you're growing. Use these question prompts to help you reflect with intention:

- ► What do I now understand or do differently because of this journey?
- ► How has this topic or skill influenced other areas of my life?
- ► What mistakes did I learn from?
- ► Who could benefit from what I've learned?
- ► What's next? Do I want to keep building on this or start something new?

 Something Extra Podcast

- ► Maxine Clark, episode 1
- ► Elise Mitchell, episode 96
- ► Laura Padousis, episode 141
- ► Tom Ziglar, episode 253

ACKNOWLEDGMENTS

I t is an absolute joy to write this acknowledgment because it gives me the chance to say a sincere *thank-you* to everyone who has been part of this incredible journey. Without your love, encouragement, and support, this project would never have come to life.

First and foremost, I give all glory to Jesus, my Lord and Savior. Without You, I am nothing and can do nothing. You are the One who makes all things possible.

To my amazing family, you are my heartbeat and the "extra" in my every day.

Greg, my husband and partner in life and business, you are the most sacrificial, intelligent, generous, and godly man I know. There is no one else I would want to do life with. Thank you for cheering me on, encouraging me endlessly, and always believing in me, even when I doubted myself. Your constant refrain to "write the book" kept me moving forward. I'm so proud to call you mine.

Jordan, you were the one who first made me a mother. Your adventurous spirit, hunger for discovery, and refusal to conform inspire me. You've never settled for the status quo, and I love that about you. I can't wait to see where your path continues to lead.

Paige, you are my forever BFF. Watching you navigate life with strength and grace in the face of illness has taught me so much about resilience, faith, and trusting God even in the unknown. I'm incredibly proud of the work you and Ally are doing through Kindred Spirits Designs. Your light is reaching far and wide.

Ally, sweet girl, thank you for showing us all a better way to live. Your love, joy, and gentle spirit have transformed our entire family. Keep shining, princess. You are changing the world just by being you.

Sawyer, wow! What a remarkable young man you are. As Poppy always said, when you came along, you showed him the other 75 percent of his heart. I feel the same. We are so proud of you and can't wait to see how you make your mark on the world.

To my dear mother-in-law, **Dixie**, thank you for always loving me like a daughter. You've been cheering me on for more than five decades and have modeled what it means to be a strong, godly woman. I also honor my late father-in-law, **Nick**, who loved me unconditionally for just as long. You are deeply missed.

To my parents who are now in their heavenly home, words will never be enough. I hit the jackpot when God chose you for me. Thank you for introducing me to Jesus. That decision has made all the difference. Your love, sacrifice, and belief in me gave me the courage to fly.

To our **Technology Partners family**, how did I get so blessed to work with such extraordinary humans? Your passion, compassion, brilliance, and commitment to each other and to our clients are nothing short of inspiring. Greg and I are deeply grateful for not just what you do but for who you are.

To the *Something Extra* **podcast team**, especially you, **Jenny Heal**, I truly don't know how I'd do this without you. You've been a priceless gift in both business and life. Who else would Ally call when she's looking for me? You keep the train on the tracks with grace and a smile. I'm still trying to figure out how you do it.

To my **ROOTED sisters**, I wish I could name all six hundred of you. To my cofounder, **Cindy Owens**, you are one of the most anchored, humble, and compassionate women I know. Thank you for your wisdom and leadership. And to **Sarah**, there was no doubt you were the one to carry ROOTED forward. Your love for Jesus and for women radiates in every conversation, blog, email, and text. It's an honor to colabor with both of you in Kingdom work.

To **Dr. Rick Lytle, Dr. Richard Blackaby, Brian Wells, Jim Bechtold, Geneviève Kroeker**, and my entire **CEO Forum family**, thank you for nearly fifteen years of wisdom, teaching, equipping, and encouragement. So many pivotal moments in our lives have stemmed from your influence. Words fall short. Let's keep transforming and impacting lives together.

There are a vast number of people who have been lifetime friends who have contributed to my growth and perspectives in life, and I am beyond grateful for each of you.

To our *Something Extra* **podcast guests**, thank you for generously sharing your wisdom, lessons, and stories with the world. I'm honored you said yes.

To the incredible team at **StoryBuilders—Josiah, Jesse, Jen, Nita, Kat, and Lainey**—this book would not exist without you. You made the process joyful and seamless, and I loved every step of the journey with you.

And finally, to **you**, the reader, thank you for walking this journey with me. My deepest hope is that through these words you will uncover your strengths, unlock your potential, and unleash your impact. May we make an eternal difference—together.

ABOUT THE AUTHOR

Lisa Nichols is the cofounder and CEO of Technology Partners, the company she and her husband, Greg, founded in 1994 with a shared vision to do business differently—grounded in transparency, partnership, and purpose. With the support of an exceptional team, they've grown Technology Partners into one of the Midwest's most respected technology firms, delivering premier IT talent, innovative solutions, and leadership development across a wide range of industries. The company has received multiple Top Workplace awards, been recognized for work-life flexibility, and consistently ranked among the region's most innovative businesses.

Lisa is also the creator and host of *Something Extra*, a top-ranked leadership podcast inspired by her daughter Ally, whose Down syndrome reminds the Nichols family that every person carries a God-given "something extra" to offer the world. What began as a tribute has evolved into a globally respected platform exploring the intersection of leadership, faith, innovation, and purpose.

Through warm, thoughtful conversations with values-driven leaders across business, technology, education, and nonprofit sectors, *Something Extra* delves into the defining moments and convictions that shape today's most impactful professionals. With over 340 episodes, the show features everyone from C-suite veterans to emerging changemakers, offering reflections on digital transformation, servant leadership, resilience, and more. Each episode is marked by Lisa's authentic voice, her deep commitment to Christian values, and her passion for helping others grow.

More than a podcast, *Something Extra* reflects Technology Partners' broader mission to elevate leadership with purpose, bridge technology and humanity, and strengthen connection with partners and communities around the world. It's become a trusted source of inspiration and insight for those who want to lead not just with excellence—but with heart.

A servant leader at her core, Lisa invests her time and energy in causes that uplift and empower others. She is active in CEO Forum, The Rooted Sisters, YPO Christian Fellowship, and the Down Syndrome Association, and has held leadership roles for YWCA, Junior Achievement, Go Red for Women, Independence Center, STAGES St. Louis, and others. Whether rallying a board, hosting a fundraiser, or sharing encouragement online, Lisa leads with integrity—believing that every win is a shared one.

She is the proud wife of Greg, mom to Jordan, Paige, and Ally, and "Yia Yia" to her grandson, Sawyer. The St. Louis suburbs have been home for over 40 years.

ENDNOTES

1   "Purpose: Shifting from Why to How," McKinsey & Company, April 22, 2020, https://www.mckinsey.com/capabilities/people-and-organizational-performance/our-insights/purpose-shifting-from-why-to-how.

2   Patrick L. Hill, and Nicholas A. Turiano, "Purpose in Life as a Predictor of Mortality Across Adulthood," Psychological Science 25, no. 7 (2014): 1482–1486, https://doi.org/10.1177/0956797614531799.